D1475587

THE NAKED CAPITALIST

A Review and Commentary on
Dr. Carroll Quigley's Book:

TRAGEDY AND HOPE—A History of the World In Our Time

Reviewed by W. Cleon Skousen

ISBN-13: 978-0-686-09164-6

Published by
Ensign Publishing
P.O. Box 298
Riverton, UT 84065

www.skousen2000.com

PHOTO CREDITS:
Deseret News, Salt Lake City, Utah
United Press
Associated Press

Dr. Carroll Quigley's book, *TRAGEDY AND HOPE—A HISTORY OF THE WORLD IN OUR TIME,* was published by The Macmillan Company, New York, and Collier-Macmillan Limited, London. The first printing of this 1,300 page volume was in 1966, price, $12.50.

Dr. Quigley is currently professor of history at the Foreign Service School of Georgetown University in Washington, D. C. He formerly taught at Harvard and Princeton and has done special research in the archives of France, Italy and England. He is the author of the college textbook, *Evolution of Civilizations,* and serves on the editorial board of the monthly publication, *Current History.*

WHY?

WHY DO SOME OF THE RICHEST PEOPLE IN THE
WORLD SUPPORT COMMUNISM AND SOCIALISM?
WHY WOULD THEY SUPPORT WHAT APPEARS
TO BE THE PATHWAY TO THEIR OWN DESTRUC-
TION? DR. CARROLL QUIGLEY OF HARVARD,
PRINCETON AND GEORGETOWN UNIVERSITIES
STATES THAT HE HAS BEEN ASSOCIATED WITH
MANY OF THESE DYNASTIC FAMILIES OF THE
SUPER-RICH. HE THEREFORE WRITES AS AN
AUTHORITY ON THE WORLD'S SECRET POWER
STRUCTURE. HIS ANSWERS TO THE ABOVE
QUESTIONS MAY ASTONISH YOU.

WHO IS TRYING TO TAKE OVER THE WORLD?

"I think the Communist conspiracy is merely a branch of a much bigger conspiracy!"

The above statement was made to this reviewer several years ago by Dr. Bella Dodd, a former member of the National Committee of the U. S. Communist Party.

Perhaps this is an appropriate introduction to a review of Dr. Carroll Quigley's book, *Tragedy And Hope.*

Dr. Dodd said she first became aware of some mysterious super-leadership right after World War II when the U. S. Communist Party had difficulty getting instructions from Moscow on several vital matters requiring immediate attention. The American Communist hierarchy was told that any time they had an emergency of this kind they should contact any one of three designated persons at the Waldorf Towers. Dr. Dodd noted that whenever the Party obtained instructions from any of these three men, Moscow always ratified them.

What puzzled Dr. Dodd was the fact that not one of these three contacts was a Russian. Nor were any of them Communists. In fact, all three were extremely wealthy American capitalists!

Dr. Dodd said, "I would certainly like to find out who is really running things."

This reviewer had also observed a number of strange developments which seemed to point to a conspiratorial control center higher and stronger than either Moscow or Peiping. For example, when Harry Dexter White (Under-Secretary of the U. S. Treasury during World War

1

DR. BELLA DODD

II) was discovered by the FBI to be a Soviet agent, the White House was immediately informed. But instead of being fired or arrested, Harry Dexter White was appointed as the new Executive Director of the U. S. Mission to the International Monetary Fund of the United Nations. He was also given a substantial increase in salary. J. Edgar Hoover was amazed. Attorney General Herbert Brownell, Jr. stated publicly that President Truman knew White was a Soviet spy when he made the appointment. (Quigley, *Tragedy And Hope,* p. 991)

Why would men in charge of the world's massive financial problems want an exposed Soviet agent such as Harry Dexter White to occupy such a highly important position in the World Bank? And why in the name of common sense would the President of the United States approve of such a thing? I heard both Congressmen and intelligence officers quizzically exclaiming, "What's going on?"

It was not long after this that the former chairman of the Federal Reserve Board began advocating economic aid and comfort to Communist China. His speech was all the more shocking because the American people had just been jolted by a Congressional hearing in which it had been shown with sworn testimony that the U. S. State Department had either recklessly allowed or deliberately propelled six hundred million Chinese allies into the grip of the Communist Chinese leaders. Nevertheless, here was this American capitalist (and former chairman of the Federal Reserve Board) telling a large meeting (where the reviewer was present) that the United States should immediately undertake extensive trade with Red China. Said he, "We never fight the people we trade with." I thought to myself, "Well, we certainly had to fight Japan in spite of all the oil and scrap iron we sold her just before World War II." It did not seem possible that this famous international banker would have forgotten such an elementary lesson so quickly.

A couple of years later, while visiting Central and South America, I noticed that certain well-known American banks were extremely powerful in controlling the politics and economic affairs of many Latin American countries. But what was baffling about it was the fact that the political regimes which these American banks supported were often virtual dictators who promoted socialism and engaged in the confiscation of privately owned industries, including American industries. Many of these bank-sponsored regimes were also openly pro-Communist.

While visiting Paraguay, I asked a man I had known for several years and who was manager of the principal American bank in Paraguay, why his bank supported a dictatorship. "Stability," he replied. "These developing countries need stability." Yet I noticed that this dictator was wiping out wealth-producing industries operating under private enterprise and placing everything under government ownership or tight socialist control.

Why was an American-owned bank financing a hard-core socialist regime? Wherever I had friends who knew the inside story in Latin American political circles, they verified the fact that the massive swing to the Left in Central and South America was being financed by certain American banks. It just didn't make sense.

Politics in Washington were equally puzzling. Why were so many top government officials always members of the Democratic Socialist cadre called Americans for Democratic Action (ADA), or were members of the exclusive Council on Foreign Relations? Whether the President was Roosevelt, Truman, Eisenhower, Kennedy, Johnson or Nixon, it seemed to make no difference. There was often a change of personalities, but membership in these two organizations seemed a prerequisite for many top government jobs.

Another puzzle was the fact that whenever the political blunders of these high-powered people aroused the anger of the public, they were not only allowed to quietly resign, but were given extremely lucrative outside jobs, usually in one of the tax-exempt foundations. It didn't look like government "of the people" but government by certain people.

I was reminded of the words of Benjamin Disraeli: "The world is governed by very different personages from what is imagined by those who are NOT behind the scenes." I began to wonder if there might not be something to the British Intelligence Digest reports which claimed that there is a small but powerful control group behind the scenes which is extremely influential in manipulating world events. The Digest seemed to have inside contacts with this group and therefore avoided identifying them by name. It simply referred to the control center as "Force X."

Professional investigators of criminal conspiracies will tell you that no matter how carefully these conspiracies are organized, they do not remain secret for long because eventually somebody on the inside becomes dissatisfied or abused and goes to the authorities with facts which can be independently verified. Political conspiracies also have a way of reaching the public, because someone on the inside is willing to tell the story. I have waited for thirty years for somebody on the inside of the modern political power structure to talk. At last, somebody has.

DR. CARROLL QUIGLEY WRITES A BOOK ON THE WORLD'S SECRET POWER STRUCTURE

Dr. Carroll Quigley is a professor of history at the Foreign Service School of Georgetown University. He formerly taught at Princeton and Harvard. He has done research in the archives of France, Italy and England. He is the author of the widely known text, *Evolution of Civilizations.*

When Dr. Quigley decided to write his 1,300 page book called *Tragedy And Hope,* he knew he was deliberately exposing one of the best kept secrets in the world. As one of the elite "insiders," he knew the scope of this power complex and he knew that its leaders hope to eventually attain total global control. Furthermore, Dr. Quigley makes it clear throughout his book that by and large he warmly supports the goals and purposes of the "network." But if that is the case, why would he want to expose this world-wide conspiracy and disclose many of its most secret operations? Obviously, disclosing the existence of a mammoth power network which is trying to take over the world could not help but arouse the vigorous resistance of the millions of people who are its intended victims. So why did Dr. Quigley write this book?

His answer appears in a number of places but is especially forceful and clear on pages 979-980. He says, in effect, that it is now too late for the little people to turn back the tide. In a spirit of kindness he is therefore urging them not to fight the noose which is already around their necks. He feels certain that those who do will only choke themselves to death. On the other hand, those who go along with the immense pressure which is beginning to be felt by all humanity will eventually find themselves in a man-made millennium of peace and prosperity. All through his book, Dr. Quigley assures us that we can trust these benevolent, well-meaning men who are secretly operating behind the scenes. THEY are the *hope* of the world. All who resist them represent *tragedy*. Hence, the title for his book.

To assure us of his own unique qualification for the writing of this book, Dr. Quigley states:

"I know of the operations of this network because I have studied it for twenty years and was permitted for two years, in the early 1960's, to examine its papers and secret records. I HAVE NO AVERSION TO IT OR TO MOST OF ITS AIMS AND HAVE, FOR MUCH OF MY LIFE, BEEN CLOSE TO IT AND TO MANY OF ITS INSTRUMENTS. I have objected, both in the past and recently, to a few of its policies . . . but in general my chief difference of opinion is that IT WISHES TO REMAIN UNKNOWN, and I believe its role in history is significant enough to be known." (p. 950, emphasis added)

Anyone reading Dr. Quigley's *Tragedy And Hope* will have little difficulty detecting the tremendous self-esteem of the author. He considers himself not only an "insider" but a member of the intellectual elite among the insiders. He feels that the forces of total global control are now sufficiently entrenched so that they can reveal their true identity without fear of being successfully overturned. He expresses the utmost contempt for members of the American middle class who think they can preserve what he calls their "petty-bourgeois" property rights and constitutional privileges. (See, for example, p. 1248)

He also expresses contempt for those who thought the Communist conspiracy was the real center of collectivized conspiracy. He ridicules their conclusions (see p. 949), and then turns right around and admits that their conclusions were correct—American anti-Communists had merely erred in knowing whom to blame. (See pp. 950-956)

Although he is a brilliant compiler, it becomes quite apparent from the start that Dr. Quigley's book is not intended to be objective. He himself boasts (as we saw in the quotation above) of his inside position with the "network," and this book is designed to portray modern history the way the network wants it told. However, as we have also noted in the previous quotation, Dr. Quigley admits he is telling more than his comrades-in-arms would care to have disclosed. They want their conspiratorial subversion to be kept a secret. Dr. Quigley thinks it is time people knew who was running things.

We see no reason to question the basic historicity of the way Dr. Quigley says the world-wide conspiratorial network developed, since these facts can be verified from other sources. We note, however, that his interpretation of modern historical events is often seriously biased by expressions of opinion or uninhibited ridicule. In dealing with recent critical issues, he is often careful to deliberately ignore many important historical facts and fails to quote the factual conclusions brought out by the bi-partisan Congressional investigations.

The real value of *Tragedy And Hope* is not so much as a "history of the world in our time" (as its subtitle suggests), but rather as a bold and boastful admission by Dr. Quigley that there actually exists a relatively small but powerful group which has succeeded in acquiring a choke-hold on the affairs of practically the entire human race.

Of course, we should be quick to recognize that no small group could wield such gigantic power unless millions of people in all walks of life were "in on the take" and were willing to knuckle down to the iron-clad regimentation of the ruthless bosses behind the scenes. As we shall see, the network has succeeded in building its power structure by using tremendous quantities of money (together with the vast influence it buys) to manipulate, intimidate, or corrupt millions of men and women and their institutions on a world-wide basis.

PERHAPS WE SHOULD HAVE ANTICIPATED JUST SUCH A DEVELOPMENT

Anyone familiar with the writings of John's Apocalypse might have suspected that modern history would eventually contain the account of a gigantic complex of political and economic power which would cover the whole earth.

John predicted that before the great epic of Messianic or Millennial peace, the human race would be subjected to a ruthless, world-wide conglomorate of dictatorial authority which would attempt to make all men subservient to it or be killed (Revelations 13:15). He said it would compel all men, "both small and great, rich and poor, free and bond," to be identified with it (Rev. 13:16).

John also referred to its economic grip on humanity and said that unless a person were identified with its monopoly network, "no man might buy or sell" (13:17).

Dr. Quigley assures us that this type of global power structure is

6

on the verge of becoming a total reality. He points out that during the past two centuries when the peoples of the world were gradually winning their political freedom from the dynastic monarchies, the major banking families of Europe and America were actually reversing the trend by setting up new dynasties of political control through the formation of international financial combines.

Dr. Quigley points out that these banking dynasties had learned that all governments must have sources of revenue from which to borrow in times of emergency. They had also learned that by providing such funds from their own private resources, they could make both kings and democratic leaders tremendously subservient to their will. It had proven to be a most effective means of controlling political appointments and deciding political issues.

We quote Dr. Quigley verbatim as he describes how these banker families evolved into vast, secret pockets of power. I have inserted topical sub-headings to facilitate reading.

The Banker Families Develop a Vast Network to Control High Finance and the Affairs of Governments:

"In time they brought into their financial network the provincial banking centers, organized as commercial banks and savings banks, as well as insurance companies, to form all of these into a single financial system on an international scale which manipulated the quantity and flow of money so that they were able to influence, if not control, governments on one side and industries on the other. The men who did this . . . aspired to establish dynasties of international bankers and were at least as successful at this as were many of the dynastic political rulers." (p. 51)

Introducing Some Of the Major Banking Family Dynasties:

"The greatest of these dynasties, of course, were the descendants of Meyer Amschel Rothschild (1743-1812) of Frankfort, whose male descendants, for at least two generations, generally married first cousins or even nieces. Rothschild's five sons, established at branches in Vienna, London, Naples, and Paris, as well as Frankfort, cooperated together in ways which other international banking dynasties copied but rarely excelled . . .

"The names of some of these [other] banking families are familiar to all of us and should be more so. They include Baring, Lazard, Erlanger, Warburg, Schroder, Selingman, the Speyers, Mirabaud, Mallet, Fould, and above all Rothschild and Morgan." (pp. 51-52)

Was This a Jewish Conspiracy? (A note by the reviewer)

It should be noted in passing that while the Rothschilds and certain other Jewish families cooperated together in these ventures, this was by no means a Jewish monopoly as some have alleged. Neither was it a "Jewish conspiracy." As we shall see, men of finance of many nationalities and many religious or non-religious backgrounds collaborated together to create the super-structure of economic and political power which Dr. Quigley is about to disclose. No student of the global conspiracy should fall for the Hitlerian doctrine that the root of all evil is a super "Jewish conspiracy." Nor should they fall for that long-since-discredited document, *The Protocols of the Learned Elders of Zion,* which Hitler palmed off on the German people as an authentic declaration of policy by an all-Jewish congress. The spurious origin of this document was proven decades ago and serves as an object lesson to those who are inclined to accept an over-simplified explanation for the rise of the global power structure which has snared mankind. Some would answer this by saying that the Anti-Defamation League (ADL) and certain other Jewish organizations have been in the forefront of the collectivist movement and also in the suppression of American voices seeking to warn the nation. However, this infiltration of the Jewish community is no more applicable to the Jewish people as a whole than the scurrilous left-wing activities of the National and World Councils of Churches is a reflection on all Protestants or the liberal, irreligious Catholic left-wing is a reflection on all Catholics. In studying the global conspiracy it is important to keep in mind that it was not any particular race or religion but the "passion for money and power" which has drawn the tycoons of world finance into a tightly-knit, mutual-aid society. Dr. Quigley identifies this group as the "International Bankers."

The International Bankers Are Different From Ordinary Bankers:

". . . they remained different from ordinary bankers in distinctive ways: (1) they were cosmopolitan and international; (2) they were close to governments and were particularly concerned with questions of government debts . . . (3) their interests were almost exclusively in bonds and very rarely in goods . . . (4) they were, accordingly, fanatical devotees of deflation . . . (5) they were almost equally devoted to secrecy and the secret use of financial influence in political life. These bankers came to be called 'international bankers' and, more particularly, were known as 'merchant bankers' in England, 'private bankers' in

8

France, and 'investment bankers' in the United States. In all countries they carried on various kinds of banking and exchange activities, but everywhere they were sharply distinguishable from other, more obvious, kinds of banks, such as savings banks or commercial banks." (p. 52)

How the Centers Of Monetary Power Were Kept Secret:

"One of their less obvious characteristics was that they remained as private unincorporated firms, usually partnerships, until relatively recently, offering no shares, no reports, and usually no advertising to the public. This risky status, which deprived them of limited liability, was retained, in most cases, until modern inheritance taxes made it essential to surround such family wealth with the immortality of corporate status for tax avoidance purposes. This persistence as private firms continued because it ensured the maximum of anonymity and secrecy to persons of tremendous public power who dreaded public knowledge of their activities as an evil almost as great as inflation. As a consequence, ordinary people had no way of knowing the wealth or areas of operation of such firms, and often were somewhat hazy as to their membership. Thus, people of considerable political knowledge might not associate the names of Walter Burns, Clinton Dawkins, Edward Grenfell, Willard Straight, Thomas Lamont, Dwight Morrow, Nelson Perkins, Russell Leffingwell, Elihu Root, John W. Davis, John Foster Dulles, and S. Parker Gilbert with the name "Morgan," yet all these and many others were parts of the system of influence which centered on the J. P. Morgan office at 23 Wall Street. This firm, like others of the international banking fraternity, constantly operated through corporations and governments. . . ." (pp. 52-53)

The Campaign to Keep Governments From Controlling Their Own Money Systems:

"The influence of financial capitalism and of the international bankers who created it was exercised both on business and on governments, but could have done neither if it had not been able to persuade both of these to accept two "axioms" of its own ideology. Both of these were based on the assumption that politicians were too weak and too subject to temporary popular pressures to be trusted with control of the money system. . . . To do this it was necessary to conceal, or even to mislead, both governments and people about the nature of money and its methods of operation." (p. 53)

9

THE ROTHSCHILDS—
ONE OF THE OLDEST BANKING DYNASTIES

The founder of the famous Rothschild dynasty was Mayer Amschel Rothschild (1743-1812) of Frankfurt, Germany. Although destined originally to be a rabbi, he became highly successful in a number of commercial pursuits and eventually established his famous banking house in Frankfurt with his five sons. Four of these sons were later sent to Vienna, London, Paris and Naples, to set up branches of their family bank. This combine soon became the most powerful banking establishment in Europe.

AMSCHEL ROTHSCHILD (the eldest son) remained in Frankfurt with his father. Eventually he became the Treasurer of the German Confederation.

SALOMON, the second son, founder of the Vienna branch. He became a leading personality in the Austro-Hungarian Empire.

NATHAN, the third son, founder of the London branch. He became the most powerful man in England.

CARL, the fourth son, who founded the Naples branch and became one of the most powerful men in Italy.

JAMES (Jacob), the fifth son, who founded the Paris branch and soon dominated the financial destiny of France.

11

The Private Bankers Decide to Set Up the Bank Of England As a Means Of Creating Credit Out Of Nothing:

"Credit has been known to the Italians and Netherlanders long before it became one of the instruments of English world supremacy. Nevertheless, the founding of the Bank of England by William Paterson and his friends in 1694 is one of the great dates in world history. For generations men had sought to avoid the one draw-back of gold, its heaviness, by using pieces of paper to represent specific pieces of gold. Today we call such pieces of paper gold certificates. Such a certificate entitles its bearer to exchange it for its piece of gold on demand, but in view of the convenience of paper, only a small fraction of certificate holders ever did make such demands. It early became clear that gold need be held on hand ONLY to the amount needed to cover the FRACTION of certificates likely to be presented for payment; accordingly, the rest of the gold could be used for business purposes, or, what amounts to the same thing, a volume of certificates could be issued GREATER than the volume of gold reserved for payment. ...Such an excess volume of paper claims against reserves we now call bank notes.

"In effect, this creation of paper claims greater than the reserves available means that bankers were creating money out of nothing. The same thing could be done in another way. .... Deposit bankers discovered that orders and checks drawn against DEPOSITS by depositors and given to a third person were often not cashed by the latter but were deposited to their own accounts. Thus there were no actual movements of funds, and payments were made simply by bookkeeping transactions on the accounts. Accordingly, it was necessary for the banker to keep on hand in actual money (gold, certificates, and notes) no more than the FRACTION of deposits likely to be drawn upon *and cashed;* the rest could be used for loans, and if these loans were made by creating a deposit [account] for the borrower, who in turn would draw checks upon it rather than withdraw it in money, such 'created deposits' or loans could also be covered adequately by retaining reserves to only a FRACTION of their value. Such created deposits also were a creation of money out of nothing, although bankers usually refused to express their actions, either note issuing or deposit lending, in these terms. William Paterson, however, on obtaining the charter of the Bank of England in 1694, to use the moneys he had won in privateering, said, 'The bank hath benefit of interest on all moneys which it creates out of nothing.'" (pp. 48-49, emphasis added)

The Bank Of England Becomes the Secret Center Of Political Power:

"In government the power of the Bank of England was a considerable restriction on political action as early as 1819 but an effort to break this power by a modification of the bank's charter in 1844 failed. In 1852, Gladstone, then Chancellor of the Exchequer and later prime minister, declared, 'The hinge of the whole situation was this: the government itself was not to be a substantive power in matters of Finance, but was to leave the Money Power supreme and unquestioned.'

"This power of the Bank of England and of its governor was admitted by most qualified observers. In January, 1924, Reginald McKenna, who had been Chancellor of the Exchequer in 1915-1916, as chairman of the board of the Midland Bank told its stock-holders: 'I am afraid the ordinary citizen will not like to be told that the banks can, and do, create money. . . . And they who control the credit of the nation direct the policy of Governments and hold in the hollow of their hands THE DESTINY OF THE PEOPLE.' In that same year, Sir Drummond Fraser, vice-president of the Institute of Bankers, stated, 'The Governor of the Bank of England must be the autocrat who dictates the terms upon which alone the Government can obtain borrowed money.'" (p. 325, emphasis added)

Concerning the Dynastic Powers Secretly Entrenched Behind British Financial Life:

"Although this situation is changing slowly, the inner circle of English financial life remains a matter of 'whom one knows,' rather than 'what one knows.' Jobs are still obtained by family, marriage, or school connections; character is considered far more important than knowledge or skill; and important positions, on this basis, are given to men who have no training, experience, or knowledge to qualify them.

"As part of this system and at the core of English financial life have been seventeen private firms of 'merchant bankers' who find money for established and wealthy enterprises. . . . These merchant bankers, WITH A TOTAL OF LESS THAN A HUNDRED ACTIVE PARTNERS, include the firms of Baring Brothers, N. M. Rothschild, J. Henry Shroder, Morgan Grenfell, Hambros, and Lazard Brothers. These merchant bankers in the period of financial capitalism had a dominant position with the Bank of England and, strangely enough STILL HAVE RETAINED SOME OF THIS, DESPITE THE NATIONALIZATION OF THE BANK by the Labour government in 1946. As

13

J. P. MORGAN
With celebrated midget, Lya Graf, during Senate hearings, 1933.

late as 1961 a Baring (Lord Cromer) was named governor of the bank, and his board of directors, called the 'Court' of the bank, included representatives of Lazard, of Hambros, and of Morgan Grenfell, as well as an industrial firm (English Electric) controlled by these." (pp. 499-500, emphasis added)

Similar Financial Dynasties Developed in the United States:

"This period, 1884-1933, was the period of financial capitalism in which investment bankers moving into commercial banking and insurance on one side and into railroading and heavy industry on the other were able to mobilize enormous wealth and wield enormous economic, political and social power. Popularly known as 'Society,' or the '400' they lived a life of dazzling splendor. Sailing the ocean in great private yachts or traveling on land by private trains, they moved in a ceremonious round between their spectacular estates and town houses in Palm Beach, Long Island, the Berkshires, Newport, and Bar Harbor, assembling from their fortress-like New York residences to attend the Metropolitan Opera under the critical eye of Mrs. Astor; or gathering for business meetings of the highest strategic level in the awesome presence of J. P. Morgan himself.

"The structure of financial controls created by the tycoons of 'Big Banking' and 'Big Business' in the period 1880-1933 was of extraordinary complexity, one business fief being built on another, both being allied with semi-independent associates, the whole rearing upward into two pinnacles of economic and financial power, of which

14

one, centered in New York, was headed by J. P. Morgan and Company, and the other, in Ohio, was headed by the Rockefeller family. When these two cooperated, as they generally did, they could influence the economic life of the country to a large degree and could almost control its political life, at least on the Federal level." (pp. 71-72)

Monopolistic Financial Structure Of the American Dynasties:

"In the United States the number of billion-dollar corporations rose from one in 1909 (United States Steel, controlled by Morgan) to fifteen in 1930. The share of all corporation assets held by the 200 largest corporations rose from 32 percent in 1909 to 49 percent in 1930 and reached 57 percent in 1939. By 1930 these 200 largest corporations held 49.2 percent of the assets of all 40,000 corporations in the country ($81 billion out of $165 billion). . . . In fact, in 1930, one corporation (American Telephone and Telegraph, controlled by Morgan) had greater assets than the total wealth in twenty-one states of the Union.

"The influence of these business leaders was so great that the Morgan and Rockefeller groups acting together, or even Morgan acting alone, could have wrecked the economic system of the country. . . ." (p. 72)

AMERICAN BANKING FAMILIES DECIDE TO ORGANIZE A FEDERAL RESERVE SYSTEM

By the beginning of the Twentieth Century, the American economy had become so dynamic that the major banking dynasties found it increasingly difficult to maintain a tight control. Even the control they had so carefully kept secret was being challenged as a major political issue in national elections.

As we have previously noted, the dynastic "banker families" in England had established their monopoly control over finance by setting up the Bank of England as a privately controlled institution which had the *appearance* of an official government institution. Similar centers of financial control had been set up in France, Germany, Italy and Switzerland. Many of these European banking families had inter-married or bought their way into the American banking dynasties so it was inevitable that eventually the same device for centralized control would be set up in the United States as that which had worked so well in various European countries. The formula called for a scheme which would look like the government was taking over when in reality, the control would be solidified in the same secret group which had always held it. As Dr. Gabriel Kolko pointed out: "Ironically, contrary to the consensus of historians, it was not the existence of monopoly that caused the federal government to intervene in the economy, but the lack of it. ... In the long run, key business leaders realized they had no vested interest in a chaotic [uncontrolled] industry and economy in which not only their profits but their very existence might be challenged." (*The Triumph of Conservatism*, Quadrangle Books, Chicago, 1967, p. 4-6)

Who Were These "Key Business Leaders?"

Dr. Quigley has identified them in *Tragedy And Hope*, and Serano S. Pratt supports the Quigley position in his book entitled, *The Work of Wall Street:*

"When we speak in Wall Street of the 'private bankers,' we refer to a handful of great banking houses whose operations are on an international scale and which in the United States represent the same power that the Rothschilds have so long possessed in Europe. These houses may, like J. P. Morgan & Co., and Brown Bros. & Co., be closely allied by partnership ties to other powerful firms in other cities; and represent here the great firms and institutions of Europe, just as August Belmont & Co. have long represented the Rothschilds." (Appleton & Company, New York, 1916, p. 340)

By the turn of the century, the Rockefellers had also joined the dynastic banking families. John D. Rockefeller had purchased the Chase Bank and his brother William bought the National City Bank of New York. The Rockefeller Chase Bank was later merged with the Warburg's Manhattan Bank to form Chase-Manhattan, the most powerful financial combine in the world today.

The scheme to set up a privately-controlled Federal Reserve System was supported by all of these dynastic banking families.

THE FIRST ATTEMPT FAILS

To appreciate some of Dr. Quigley's comments in *Tragedy And Hope*, we should summarize the origin and history of the Federal Reserve System.

Stephen Birmingham (in his book, *Our Crowd*, Dell Publishing Co., New York, 1967, p. 400) says the person who played the most significant part in getting Federal Reserve adopted was Paul Warburg. He had come to the United States with his brother, Felix Warburg, from Germany in 1902. They left their brother Max in Frankfurt to run the family bank. In due time Paul married Nina Loeb of Kuhn, Loeb and Company, while Felix married Jacob Schiff's daughter, Frieda Schiff. Both brothers became Kuhn-Loeb partners and Paul was awarded a yearly salary of $500,000 to go up and down the country preparing the climate for a central banking system in the United States.

Working with Warburg was J. P. Morgan's leading Washington representative, Senator Nelson Aldrich, whose daughter Abby was married to John D. Rockefeller, Jr. (Nelson Rockefeller, governor of New York, is named after his maternal grandfather.)

Senator Aldrich and Paul Warburg set up an extremely secretive meeting with representatives of the leading banking dynasties to prepare the first draft for the Federal Reserve System. They met on Jekyl Island, Georgia. Rockefeller's agent, Frank Vanderlip admitted many years later:

"Despite my views about the value to society of greater publicity for the affairs of corporations, there was an occasion, near the close of 1910, when I was as secretive—indeed as furtive—as any conspirator. ... I do not feel it is any exaggeration to speak of our secret expedition to Jekyl Island as the occasion of the actual conception of what eventually became the Federal Reserve System." (Frank Vanderlip, "Farm Boy to Financier," *Saturday Evening Post,* February 9, 1935, p. 25)

The secret meeting on Jekyl Island included Henry P. Davison of J. P. Morgan & Company; Frank A. Vanderlip, President of the Rockefeller-owned National City Bank; A. Piatt Andrew, Assistant Secretary of the Treasury; Benjamin Strong of Morgan's Bankers Trust Company, and, of course, Paul Warburg.

This was right at the time when the idea of creating a Federal central bank *"free of Wall Street or any monopolistic interest"* was being promoted by the *Banking Law Journal* and a number of national political personalities. Therefore, the object of the conference on Jekyl Island was to set up a central bank which had the appearance of meeting this demand while actually thwarting it. Paul Warburg went to the conference with a plan copied after the private central banks in England and Europe. Professor Kolko writes: "The plan which emerged from the conference was very much like Warburg's in principle, and Warburg claimed authorship for it even though Vanderlip actually drafted the final plan." (*Op. Cit.,* p. 184)

But the plan failed. It was introduced into the Senate as the Aldrich Bill. The name of Aldrich was so closely linked to Morgan and

Wall Street, and the resentment against these influences was so strong, that the bill was readily defeated. The group of master planners backed away to devise a new tactic.

THE FEDERAL RESERVE SYSTEM FINALLY BECOMES A REALITY

It was decided that the Republican Party was too closely connected with Wall Street and the only hope of getting a central bank adopted would be to get the Democrats in power and have a new bill introduced which would be promoted into popular acceptance by claiming that it was a measure designed to strip Wall Street of its power. The Wall Street cadre thereupon set forth to achieve this in the presidential election of 1912.

At first this looked virtually impossible, because President William Howard Taft (a Republican who had opposed the Aldrich Bill) was very popular and seemed a sure-fire bet for re-election. The picture changed when the former President Teddy Roosevelt (also a Republican but opposed to Taft) decided to run on the Progressive Party ticket against Taft. The Democrats then nominated Woodrow Wilson, making it a three-way race. Suddenly the central bank promoters saw the opportunity they needed.

Two Morgan agents, Frank Munsey and George Perkins moved in behind Teddy Roosevelt with money and manpower from Wall Street. As Ferdinand Lundberg states:

"As soon as Roosevelt signified that he would again challenge Taft, the President's defeat was inevitable. Throughout the three-cornered fight Roosevelt had Munsey and Perkins constantly at his heels, supplying money, going over his speeches, bringing people from Wall Street in to help, and, in general, carrying the entire burden of the campaign against Taft. . . .

"Perkins and J. P. Morgan and Company were the substance of the Progressive Party; everything else was trimming. . . . In short, most of Roosevelt's campaign fund was supplied by the two Morgan hatchet men who were seeking Taft's scalp." (*America's 60 Families*, the Vanguard Press, New York, 1938, pp. 110-112)

Meanwhile, Wall Street was ALSO backing Wilson. Clear back in 1906, George Harvey, president of the Morgan-controlled *Harper's Weekly*, had suggested Wilson for President. Then the Rockefellers took up the fund-raising for Wilson together with other Wall Street

BERNARD BARUCH CHATTING WITH PRESIDENT EISENHOWER

backers of the Democratic Party. Ferdinand Lundberg says:

"The financial genius behind Woodrow Wilson was Cleveland H. Dodge of the [Rockefeller] National City Bank. ... Sitting with Dodge as co-directors of the National City Bank at the time were the younger Rockefeller, J. Ogden Armour, and James Stillman. In short, except for George F. Baker, everyone whom the Pujo Committee (in Congress) had termed rulers of the 'Money Trust' was in this bank." (*Op. Cit.,* pp. 109-113)

Additional supporters of Wilson who belonged to the dynastic banking families included Jacob Schiff, Bernard Baruch, Henry Morgenthau, Thomas Fortune Ryan, and the publisher of the *New York Times,* Adolph Ochs. (Kolko, *Op. Cit.,* pp. 205 and 211)

Even Morgan's men who managed Teddy Roosevelt's campaign had money behind Wilson. The idea was to give Roosevelt enough support to divide Taft's Republican vote and give Wilson enough support to beat them both. This strategy worked, and Wilson was elected.

Even before the election, however, the promoters of the central bank set up a front organization to create a public climate which would be favorable to the Federal Reserve idea. Professor Kolko says:

19

PRESIDENT WILSON, MRS. WILSON AND "COL." EDWARD M. HOUSE

"During the spring of 1911 the backers of the plan moved to create the 'National Citizens League for the Promotion of a Sound Banking System' to accomplish the task. Warburg and the other New York bankers behind the Aldrich plan arranged to have the league centered in Chicago. . . ." (*Op. Cit.,* p. 186)

Because of the Rockefeller influence over the University of Chicago, this new front organization was headed by J. Lawrence Laughlin of that institution with his former student and close confidante, H. Parker Willis, writing the necessary legislation. It was simply the Aldrich Bill in a new dress.

To see that the newly elected President would have the right advisors, Wilson's financial backers surrounded him with their own agents. The most important of these was "Colonel" Edward Mandell House, the British-educated son of a financier who represented certain British financial interests in the Southern States. House gradually emerged as the virtual president during the Wilson administration. Two of his pet projects, the central bank and the graduated income tax, were both successfully adopted through the amazing capacity of House to pull wires behind the scenes. It is now known that House was the author of the book, *Philip Dru: Administrator,* which described how

Dru worked to establish "Socialism as dreamed by Karl Marx."

Professor Charles Seymour who edited *The Intimate Papers of Colonel House,* assures us that House was the "unseen guardian angel" of the Federal Reserve Act. There was constant contact between House and Paul Warburg. The biographer for House assures us further that "The Schiffs, the Warburgs, the Kahns, the Rockefellers, and the Morgans had faith in House. ..."

To prevent opponents of Wall Street from identifying the Federal Reserve Act with the international bankers, a smoke-screen of opposition was fulminated. In his autobiography, William McAdoo, Wilson's Secretary of the Treasury and son-in-law, wrote:

"Bankers fought the Federal Reserve legislation—and every provision of the Federal Reserve Act—with the tireless energy of men fighting a forest fire. They said it was populistic, socialistic, half-baked, destructive, infantile, badly conceived and unworkable." (p. 213)

However, McAdoo talked with these heated opponents of President Wilson's Federal Reserve project and decided there might be something phoney about the smoke-screen of opposition. "These interviews with bankers led me to an interesting conclusion. I perceived gradually, through all the haze and smoke of controversy, that the banking world was not really as much opposed to the bill as it pretended to be. ..." (p. 225)

Thus the stage was set. It was December 22, 1913, that the Federal Reserve Act passed the House of Representatives by a vote of 298 to 60 and the Senate passed it by a majority of 43 to 25.

BUT WHO CONTROLS THE FEDERAL RESERVE SYSTEM?

The operation of the Federal Reserve System is one of the most interesting and mysterious combines in the country. Since it was founded in 1913 it has successfully resisted every attempt to conduct an audit of its affairs. The system consists of 12 "National Banks" but the only one of any significance is the one in New York. The New York bank has always been managed by someone completely congenial to the interests of the international bankers. It is important to realize that the Federal Reserve System is not a bona fide Government agency. Technically the stock is owned by the 12 National Banks which receive a dividend of six percent each year. Any profits from the System are supposed to be turned over to the U. S. Treasury. In fact, the President appoints the seven members of the Federal Reserve Board for fourteen-year terms, but in spite of all this window dressing the Federal Reserve Board is completely independent in its decisions. President Johnson admitted this when the Federal Reserve defied him during his administration and when David Kennedy, the Nixon Secretary of the treasury, was asked about the credit-tightening policies of the Federal Reserve, he replied: "It's not my job to approve or disapprove. It is the action of the Federal Reserve." (*U. S. News and World Report,* May 5, 1969)

The mammoth and secret operations of the Federal Reserve are therefore proceeding along the lines which Dr. Quigley says the international bankers were determined to achieve. They intended to use the financial power of Britain and the United States to force all the major countries to operate "through central banks free from all political control, with all questions of international finance to be settled by agreements by such central banks without interference from governments." (Quigley, p. 326)

The motivation for such a scheme can be better appreciated when it is realized that loaning money to governments can be a very lucrative business, especially loans to the United States Government. The U. S. presently owes more money (most of it to the international banking institutions) than all the money owed by the rest of the nations in the world combined. The U. S. national debt is presently 372 billion dollars. EVERY YEAR American tax payers are required to contribute 20 billion dollars to pay the interest on this indebtedness. It is the third largest item in the Federal budget. It can be readily seen why those who are appointed to the key positions in the U. S. Federal Reserve System (where loans are negotiated and interest rates fixed) occupy possibly the most critically influential spot in the entire world.

Dr. Quigley says the true dimensions of the whole scheme are better appreciated when it is realized that the far-reaching aim of the dynastic bankers was:

". . . nothing less than to create a world system of financial control in private hands able to dominate the POLITICAL SYSTEM of each country and the ECONOMY of the world as a whole. This system was to be controlled in a feudalist fashion by the central banks of the world acting in concert, by secret agreements arrived at in frequent private meetings and conferences. The apex of the system was to be the Bank for International Settlements in Basle, Switzerland, a private bank owned and controlled by the world's central banks which were themselves private corporations. Each central bank, in the hands of men like Montague Norman of the Bank of England, Benjamin Strong of the New York Federal Reserve Bank, Charles Rist of the Bank of France, and Hjalmer Schacht of the Reichs bank, sought to dominate its government by its ability to control Treasury loans, to manipulate foreign exchanges, to influence the level of economic activity in the country, and to influence cooperative politicians by subsequent economic rewards in the business world." (p. 324, emphasis added)

That the international bankers have been in complete control of the U. S. Federal Reserve System from its inception is readily demonstrated. Dr. Quigley points out that the first governor of the Federal Reserve Bank of New York was Benjamin Strong, who became a close colleague of Montague Norman of the Bank of England.

"Strong owed his career to the favor of the Morgan Bank, especially of Henry P. Davison, who made him secretary of the Bankers Trust Company of New York (in succession to Thomas W. Lamont) in 1904, used him as Morgan's agent in the banking rearrangements following the crash of 1907, and made him vice-president of the Bankers Trust (still in succession to Lamont) in 1909. He became governor of the Federal Reserve Bank of New York as the joint nominee of Morgan and of Kuhn, Loeb and Company in 1914. Two years later, Strong met Norman for the first time, and they at once made an agreement to work in cooperation for the financial practices they both revered." (p. 326)

The original Federal Reserve Board was largely hand-picked by "Colonel" House and included Paul Warburg. Subsequent appointments have always been completely congenial to the interests of Wall Street and the international bankers. Ferdinand Lundberg confirms Quigley's evaluations:

"In practice the Federal Reserve Bank of New York became the fountainhead of the system of twelve regional banks, for New York was the money market of the nation. The other eleven banks were so many expensive mausoleums erected to salve the local pride and quell the Jacksonian fears of the Hinterland. Benjamin Strong . . . president of the Bankers Trust Company [Morgan], was selected as the first Governor of the New York Reserve Bank. An adept in high finance, Strong for many years manipulated the country's monetary system at the discretion of directors representing the leading New York banks. Under Strong the Reserve System, unsuspected by the nation, was brought into interlocking relations with the Bank of England and the Bank of France. . . ." (*Op. Cit.*, p. 122)

So now we have run full circle. Dr. Carroll Quigley was anxious to have us know who has been running the world. He makes it clear that in spite of their power, these secret centers of control are seldom in dictatorial positions where they can actually take direct, decisive political action; but their financial stranglehold on the world allows them to INFLUENCE and MANIPULATE the affairs of various nations to an amazing degree and to suit their own purposes. Therefore, whatever the purposes and goals of this group happen to be are of monumental importance to the rest of the world.

WHAT ARE THE GOALS OF THE WORLD'S SECRET POWER MANIPULATORS?

Having established how powerful the money-managers of the world have now become, Dr. Quigley's second purpose appears to have been his desire to let us know what the political philosophy of these world giants has turned out to be. This is undoubtedly the most shocking aspect of his book. It is all the more disturbing because the facts in this part of his book fit perfectly with the world of reality in which we find ourselves. Many things which have seemed inconsistent and incongruous suddenly loom up with startling clarity as Dr. Quigley provides an insider's analysis of what has been happening.

In the beginning of this presentation I pointed out, some of the disturbing questions which are likely to occur to anyone who has been trying to understand the significance of the amazing trends of current history. There is a growing volume of evidence that the highest centers of political and economic power have been forcing the entire human race toward a global, socialist, dictatorial-oriented society. And what has been *most* baffling about it has been the fact that this drift toward dictatorship with its inevitable obliteration of a thousand years of struggle toward human freedom, is being plotted, promoted and implemented by the leaders of free nations and the super-rich of those nations whose positions of affluence would seem to make them the foremost beneficiaries of the free-enterprise, property-oriented, open society in which so much progress has been made. Certainly they, above all men, should know that in order for this system to survive, freedom of action and the integrity of property rights must be preserved. Then why are the super-capitalists trying to destroy them?

Dr. Quigley provides an answer to this question but it is so startling that at first it seems virtually inconceivable. It becomes rational only as his scattered references to it are collected and digested point by point. In a nutshell, Dr. Quigley has undertaken to expose what every insider like himself has known all along—that the world hierarchy of the dynastic super-rich is out to take over the entire planet, doing it with Socialistic legislation where possible, but having no reluctance to use Communist revolution where necessary.

As we shall observe shortly, Dr. Quigley is sometimes reluctant to admit the full ramifications of his ugly thesis when the shocking and often revolting implications of it spill out on the blood-stained pages of recent history. This is why we find him proving his thesis up to a point and then frantically endeavoring to cover up the consequences of it by denying the validity of what Congressional Committees have exposed through their investigations. This black thread of strange contradiction runs through several important sections of Dr. Quigley's book, but should offer no difficulty to the reader once he understands what is happening.

As we pointed out earlier, Dr. Quigley prides himself in being a member of this secret power group which is identified with the international jet-set of super-rich banking dynasties. He agrees with practically all of their goals and policies. However, he strongly objects to their policy of secrecy. (p. 950) He wants them to receive credit for what they have been doing. He therefore undertakes to show who has been largely responsible for the massive movement toward the collectivizing of power on the Socialist-Communist Left during the past fifty to seventy-five years.

It began with the ideological conquest of some important people's minds.

DR. QUIGLEY'S EXPLANATION OF AN AMAZING PHENOMENON

The ancient political philosophers knew that the most effective way to conquer a man is to capture his mind. There is no slave more devoted nor disciple more dedicated than the man who has become completely obsessed with the vision of what he considers to be a great idea. Dr. Quigley says this is what has happened to the leaders of the world's secret center of international banking. Its leaders became convinced that they had come upon a fantastically great idea: How to take over and control the resources of the world for the good of humanity.

Here is how Dr. Quigley says it all began.

The Coming Of John Ruskin To Oxford:

"Until 1870 there was no professorship of fine arts at Oxford, but in that year, thanks to the Slade bequest, John Ruskin was named to such a chair. He hit Oxford like an earthquake, not so much because he talked about fine arts, but because he talked also about the empire and England's downtrodden masses, and above all because he talked about all three of these things as moral issues." (p. 130)

Who Was John Ruskin? (Reviewer's note):

We need to pause for a moment to get better acquainted with John Ruskin so we can better appreciate what Dr. Quigley has to say about him. John Ruskin (1819-1900) was born in London, the son of a wealthy wine merchant from whom he inherited a substantial fortune. His education was in art, literature, architecture, mathematics, Latin and Greek. He traveled widely, graduated from Oxford, and in 1870 became the Slade professor of art at his alma mater. However, art was only a partial interest. He had his students build roads and venture out into a variety of community experiments. He established the "St. George's Guild" which was designed to set up a model industrial and social movement, to buy lands, mills and factories, and to start a model industry or cooperative on socialist lines. The Guild failed, but as Dr. Quigley will point out shortly, the ideas of Ruskin were planted in the fertile minds of his students who were the scions of the British aristocracy.

What were his ideas? Kenneth Clark, in his *Ruskin Today* (Holt, Rinehart and Winston, New York, 1964) says: "He saw that the state must take control of the means of production and distribution, and organize them for the good of the community as a whole; but he was prepared to place the control of the state in the hands of a single man. 'My continual aim has been to show the eternal superiority of some men to others, sometimes even of one man to all others.' He had a very low opinion of democracy, and what he thought of freedom may be found in the passage . . . on the house-fly. These views are not at present accepted in the English-speaking world; and it must be admitted that the experiences of the last thirty years have done little to recommend them. No doubt Ruskin underrated the corruptibility of man and the coarseness inherent in all forms of government. He would have been horrified by the exploits of Hitler and Stalin. But I doubt if he would have shrunk from the results of his doctrine as much as one would suppose. In spite of its materialist philosophy, he would, I think, have approved of Communism; the peasant communes in China, in particular, are exactly on his model. He would not have thought the cure worse than the disease because he could not imagine a worse disease than the capitalist society of the nineteenth century." (pp. 267-268)

John Ruskin, Clark tells us, derived most of his ideas and inspiration "directly from the source book of all dictatorships, Plato's *Republic*. He read Plato almost every day. . . ." (p. 269) Of course Marx, Engels, Proudhon and Saint-Simon drank from that same fountain. Therefore, there is a remarkable

JOHN RUSKIN

parallel in the writings of Ruskin, Marx and other disciples of Plato. Plato wanted a ruling class with a powerful army to keep it in power and a society completely subordinate to the monolithic authority of the rulers. He also advocated using whatever force was necessary for the wiping out of all existing government and social structure so the new rulers could begin with a "clean canvas" on which to develop the portrait of their great new society.

The upper dimensions of Plato's "ideal" society included the elimination of marriage and the family so that all the women would belong to all the men and all the men would belong to all the women. Children resulting from these promiscuous unions would be taken over by the government as soon as they were weaned and raised anonymously by the state. Plato wanted women to be required to be equal with men —to fight wars with the men and perform labor like men. There was to be selective breeding of men and women under control of the government and children considered inferior or crippled were to be destroyed. There was to be a three-level structure of society into fixed classes: the ruling class, the military class and the worker class. Plato said the people would be induced to believe a government-indoctrinated falsehood that people were born with gold, silver or copper in their souls and the rulers would determine which metal was present in the soul of each person and assign him to the appropriate class. Plato admitted all this was a falsehood but said it would facilitate the administration of affairs by the rulers because it would be taught to the people as a religious principle. Plato reserved the full blessings of communism for his ruling class. It would be there that he felt private property could be eliminated, family relations communalized, and intellectual energy devoted to determining what was good for the masses in the lower classes.

All this was part of what John Ruskin read "almost every day." Now we will continue with Dr. Quigley's analysis of what happened when John Ruskin "hit Oxford like an earthquake."

Ruskin Taught That the Ruling Class Of England Had a World Mission:

"Ruskin spoke to the Oxford undergraduates as members of the privileged, ruling class. He told them that they were the possessors of a magnificent tradition of education, beauty, rule of law, freedom, decency, and self-discipline but that this tradition could not be saved, and did not deserve to be saved, unless it could be extended to the lower classes in England itself **and to the non-English masses throughout the world**. If this precious tradition were not extended to these two great majorities, the minority of upper-class Englishmen would ultimately be submerged by these majorities and the tradition lost. To prevent this, the tradition must be extended to the masses and to the empire." (p. 130, emphasis added)

Cecil Rhodes Caught the Vision Of a World-Wide Federation:

"Ruskin's message had a sensational impact. His inaugural lecture was copied out in longhand by one undergraduate, Cecil Rhodes, who kept it with him for thirty years. Rhodes (1853-1902) feverishly exploited the diamond and goldfields of South Africa, rose to be prime minister of the Cape Colony (1890-1896), contributed money to political parties, controlled parliamentary seats both in England and South Africa, and sought to win a strip of British territory across Africa from the Cape of Good Hope to Egypt and to join these two extremes together with a telegraph line and ultimately with a Cape-to-Cairo Railway. Rhodes inspired devoted support for his goals from others in South Africa and in England. With financial support from Lord Rothschild and Alfred Beit, he was able to monopolize the diamond mines of South Africa as DeBeers Consolidated Mines and

CECIL RHODES ABOUT THE TIME
HE ATTENDED OXFORD

CECIL RHODES AT THE HEIGHT
OF HIS POWER

to build up a great gold mining enterprise as Consolidated Gold Fields. In the middle of the 1890's Rhodes had a personal income of at least a million pounds sterling a year (then about five million dollars) which was spent so freely for his mysterious purposes that he was usually overdrawn on his account." (p. 130)

Rhodes Launched a Long-Range Program To Federate the World:

"These purposes centered on his desire to federate the English-speaking peoples and to bring **all the habitable portions of the world** under their control. For this purpose Rhodes left part of his great fortune to found the Rhodes Scholarships at Oxford in order to spread the English ruling class tradition throughout the English-speaking world as Ruskin had wanted." (pp. 130-131, emphasis added)

Rhodes Received Wide Support and Organized a Secret Society:

"Among Ruskin's most devoted disciples at Oxford were a group of intimate friends including Arnold Toynbee, Alfred (later Lord) Milner, Arthur Glazebrook, George (later Sir George) Parkin, Philip Lyttleton Gell, and Henry (later Sir Henry) Birchenough. These were so moved by Ruskin that they devoted the rest of their lives to carrying out his ideas. A similar group of Cambridge men including Reginald Baliol Brett (Lord Esher), Sir John B. Seeley, Albert (Lord) Grey, and

29

Edmund Garrett were also aroused by Ruskin's message and devoted their lives to extension of the British Empire and uplift of England's urban masses as two parts of one project which they called 'extension of the English-speaking idea.' They were remarkably successful in these aims because England's most sensational journalist William T. Stead (1840-1912), an ardent social reformer and imperialist, brought them into association with Rhodes. This association was formally established on February 5, 1891, when Rhodes and Stead organized a secret society of which Rhodes had been dreaming for sixteen years." (p. 131)

The Original Structure of Rhodes' Secret Society:

"In this secret society Rhodes was to be leader; Stead, Brett (Lord Esher), and Milner were to form an executive committee; Arthur (Lord) Balfour, (Sir) Harry Johnston, Lord Rothschild, Albert (Lord) Grey, and others were listed as potential members of a 'Circle of Initiates'; while there was to be an outer circle known as the 'Association of Helpers' (later organized by Milner as the Round Table Organization). Brett was invited to join this organization the same day and Milner a couple of weeks later, on his return from Egypt. Both accepted with enthusiasm. Thus the central part of the secret society was established by March 1891. It continued to function as a formal group, although the outer circle was, apparently, not organized until 1909-1913." (p. 131)

The Perpetuation Of the Secret Society After Rhodes' Death:

"This group was able to get access to Rhodes' money after his death in 1902 and also to the funds of loyal Rhodes supporters like Alfred Beit (1853-1906) and Sir Abe Bailey (1864-1940). With this backing they sought to extend and execute the ideals that Rhodes had obtained from Ruskin and Stead. Milner was the chief Rhodes Trustee and Parkin was Organizing Secretary of the Rhodes Trust after 1902, while Gell and Birchenough, as well as others with similar ideas, became officials of the British South Africa Company. They were joined in their efforts by other Ruskinite friends of Stead's like Lord Grey, Lord Esher, and Flora Shaw (later Lady Lugard). In 1890, by a stratagem too elaborate to describe here, Miss Shaw became Head of the Colonial Department of *The Times* while still remaining on the Payroll of Stead's *Pall Mall Gazette.* In this post she played a major role in the next ten years in carrying into execution the imperial schemes of Cecil Rhodes, to whom Stead had introduced her in 1889." (pp. 131-32)

The Secret Society Was Gradually Extended Into Other Countries:
"As governor-general and high commissioner of South Africa in the period 1897-1905, Milner recruited a group of young men, chiefly from Oxford and from Toynbee Hall, to assist him in organizing his administration. Through his influence these men were able to win influential posts in government and international finance and became the dominant influence in British imperial and foreign affairs up to 1939. Under Milner in South Africa, they were known as Milner's Kindergarten until 1910. In 1909-1913 they organized semi-secret groups, known as Round Table Groups, in the chief British dependencies and in the United States. These still function in eight countries. They kept in touch with each other by personal correspondence and frequent visits, and through an influential quarterly magazine, *The Round Table,* founded in 1910 and largely supported by Sir Abe Bailey's money. In 1919 they founded the Royal Institute of International Affairs (Chatham House) for which the chief financial supporters were Sir Abe Bailey and the Astor family (owners of *The Times*)." (p. 132)

Forming Of the Council On Foreign Relations and the Institute Of Pacific Relations:
"Similar Institutes of International Affairs were established in the chief British dominions and in the United States (where it is known as the Council on Foreign Relations) in the period 1919-1927. After 1925 a somewhat similar structure of organizations, known as the Institute of Pacific Relations, was set up in twelve countries holding territory in the Pacific area, the units in each British dominion existing on an interlocking basis with the Round Table Group and the Royal Institute of International Affairs in the same country. In Canada the nucleus of this group consisted of Milner's undergraduate friends at Oxford (such as Arthur Glazebrook and George Parkin), while in South Africa and India the nucleus was made up of former members of Milner's Kindergarten. These included (Sir) Patrick Duncan, B. K. Long, Richard Feetham and (Sir) Dougal Malcolm in South Africa and (Sir) William Marris, James (Lord) Meston, and their friend Malcolm (Lord) Hailey in India. The groups in Australia and New Zealand had been recruited by Stead (through his magazine *The Review of Reviews)* as early as 1890-1893; by Parkin, at Milner's instigation, in the period 1889-1910, and by Lionel Curtis, also at Milner's request, in 1910-1919." (pp. 132-133)

31

How the Secret Society Gained Massive Influence in the British Government, the British Press and the British Universities:

"The power and influence of this Rhodes-Milner group in British imperial affairs and in foreign policy since 1889, although not widely recognized, can hardly be exaggerated. We might mention as an example that this group dominated *The Times* from 1890 to 1912 and has controlled it completely since 1912 (except for the years 1919-1922). Because *The Times* has been owned by the Astor family since 1922, this Rhodes-Milner group was sometimes spoken of as the 'Cliveden Set,' named after the Astor country house where they sometimes assembled. Numerous other papers and journals have been under the control or influence of this group since 1889. They have also established and influenced numerous university and other chairs of imperial affairs and international relations. Some of these are the Beit chairs at Oxford, the Montague Burton chair at Oxford, the Rhodes chair at London, the Stevenson chair at Chatham House, the Wilson chair at Aberystwyth, and others, as well as such important sources of influence as Rhodes House at Oxford." (p. 133)

The Proposal to Have the Capital Of the World Federation in the United States:

"From 1884 to about 1915 the members of this group worked valiantly to extend the British Empire and to organize it in a federal system. They were constantly harping on the lessons to be learned from the failure of the American Revolution and the success of the Canadian federation of 1867, and hoped to federate the various parts of the empire as seemed feasible, then confederate the whole of it, with the United Kingdom into a single organization. They also hoped to bring the United States into this organization to whatever degree was possible. Stead was able to get Rhodes to accept, in principle, a solution which might have made Washington the capital of the whole organization or allow parts of the empire to become states of the American Union." (p. 133)

RHODES-MILNER SECRET SOCIETY EXTENDS ITS INFLUENCE TO THE UNITED STATES

The story of how the secret society of the Rhodes-Milner axis extended its influence into the United States is summarized by Dr. Quigley as follows:

". . . the American branch of this organization (sometimes called the 'Eastern Establishment') has played a very significant role in the history of the United States in the last generation. . . . By 1915 Round Table groups existed in seven countries, including England, South Africa, Canada, Australia, New Zealand, India, and a rather loosely organized group in the United States (George Louis Beer, Walter Lippmann, Frank Aydelotte, Whitney Shepardson, Thomas W. Lamont, Jerome D. Greene, Erwin D. Canham of the *Christian Science Monitor,* and others). The attitudes of the various groups were coordinated by frequent visits and discussions and by a well-informed and totally anonymous quarterly magazine *The Round Table,* whose first issue, largely written by Philip Kerr, appeared in November 1910." (p. 950)

J. P. Morgan, Rockefeller and Other Wealthy Americans Join the Rhodes Secret Society:

"Money for the widely ramified activities of this organization came originally from the associates and followers of Cecil Rhodes, chiefly from the Rhodes Trust itself, and from wealthy associates such as the Beit Brothers, from Sir Abe Bailey, and (after 1915) from the Astor family. Since 1925 there have been substantial contributions from wealthy individuals and from foundations, and firms associated with the international banking fraternity, especially the Carnegie United Kingdom Trust, and other organizations associated with J. P. Morgan, the Rockefeller and Whitney families, and the associates of Lazard Brothers and of Morgan, Grenfell, and Company." (p. 951)

Forming Of the British-American Secret Society Alliance:

"The chief backbone of this organization grew up along the already existing financial cooperation running from the Morgan Bank in New York to a group of international financiers in London led by Lazard Brothers. Milner himself in 1901 had refused a fabulous offer, worth up to $100,000 a year, to become one of the three partners of the Morgan Bank in London, in succession to the younger J. P. Morgan who moved from London to join his father in New York (eventually the vacancy went to E. C. Grenfell, so that the London affiliate of Morgan became known as Morgan, Grenfell, and Company.) Instead, Milner became director of a number of public banks, chiefly the London Joint Stock Bank, corporate precursor of the Midland Bank. He became one of the greatest political and financial powers in England, with his disciples strategically placed throughout England in significant places, such as the editorship of *The Times,* the editorship of *The Observer,* the managing directorship of Lazard Brothers, various administrative posts, and even Cabinet positions. Ramifications were established in politics, high finance, Oxford and London universities, periodicals, the civil service, and tax-exempt foundations." (p. 951)

Implementing the American Branch Of the Secret Society:

"At the end of the war of 1914, it became clear that the organization of this system had to be greatly extended. Once again the task was entrusted to Lionel Curtis who established, in England and each dominion, a front organization to the existing local Round Table Group. This front organization, called the Royal Institute of International Affairs, had as its nucleus in each area the existing submerged Round Table Group. In New York it was known as the Council on Foreign Relations, and was a front for J. P. Morgan and Company in association with the very small American Round Table Group. The American organizers were dominated by the large number of Morgan 'experts,' including Lamont and Beer, who had gone to the Paris Peace Conference and there became close friends with the similar group of English 'experts' which had been recruited by the Milner group. In fact the original plans for the Royal Institute of International Affairs and the Council of Foreign Relations were drawn up at Paris. The Council of the RIIA (which, by Curtis' energy came to be housed in Chatham House, across St. James' Square from the Astors, and was soon known by the name of this headquarters) and the board of the Council on Foreign Relations have carried ever since the marks of their origin. Until 1960 the council at Chatham House was dominated by the dwindling group of Milner's associates, while the paid staff members were largely the agents of Lionel Curtis. *The Round Table* for years (until 1961) was edited from the back door of Chatham House grounds in Ormond Yard, and its telephone came through the Chatham House switchboard." (pp. 951-952)

The Powerful New York Branch Of the Secret Society:

"The New York branch was dominated by the associates of the Morgan Bank. For example, in 1928 the Council on Foreign Relations had John W. Davis as president, Paul Cravath as vice-president, and a council of thirteen others, which included Owen D. Young, Russell C. Leffingwell, Norman Davis, Allen Dulles, George W. Wickersham, Frank L. Polk, Whitney Shepardson, Isaiah Bowman, Stephen P. Duggan, and Otto Kahn. Throughout its history the council has been associated with the American Round Tablers, such as Beer, Lippmann, Shepardson, and Jerome Greene." (p.952)

Founding Of The New Republic Magazine:

"The best example of this alliance of Wall Street and Left-wing publication was *The New Republic,* a magazine found by Willard Straight, using Payne Whitney money, in 1914. Straight, who had been assistant to Sir Robert Hart (Director of the Chinese Imperial Customs Service and the head of the European imperialist penetration of China) had remained in the Far East from 1901 to 1912, became a Morgan partner and the firm's chief expert on the Far East. He married Dorothy Payne Whitney whose names indicate the family alliance of two of America's greatest fortunes. She was the daughter of William C. Whitney, New York Utility millionaire and the sister of coheiress of Oliver Payne, of the Standard Oil 'trust'. One of her brothers married Gertrude Vanderbilt, while the other, Payne Whitney, married the daughter of Secretary of State John Hay, who enunciated the American policy of the 'Open Door' in China. In the next generation, three first cousins, John Hay ('Jock') Whitney, Cornelius Vanderbilt ('Sonny') Whitney, and Michael Whitney ('Mike') Straight, were allied in numerous public policy enterprises of a propagandist nature, and all three served in varied roles in the late New Deal and Truman administrations. In these they were closely allied with other 'Wall Street Liberals,' such as Nelson Rockefeller. . . . The original purpose for establishing the paper [*The New Republic*] was to provide an outlet for the progressive Left and to guide it quietly in an Anglophile direction." (pp. 938-939)

Walter Lippmann and The New Republic Magazine:

"This latter task was entrusted to a young man, only four years out of Harvard, but already a member of the mysterious Round Table Group, which has played a major role in directing England's foreign policy since its formal establishment in 1909. This new recruit, Walter Lippmann, has been from 1914 to the present, the authentic spokesman in American journalism for the Establishments on both sides of the Atlantic in international affairs. His biweekly columns, which appear in hundreds of American papers, are copyrighted by the New York *Herald Tribune* which is now owned by J. H. Whitney. It was these connections as a link between Wall Street and the Round Table Group, which gave Lippmann the opportunity in 1918, while still in his twenties, to be the official interpreter of the meaning of Woodrow Wilson's Fourteen Points to the British Government." (p. 939)

35

WALTER LIPPMANN

Acquiring Influence Among Academic Institutions:

"This group, which in the United States, was completely dominated by J. P. Morgan and Company from the 1880's to the 1930's was cosmopolitan, Anglophile, internationalist, Ivy League, eastern seaboard, high Episcopalian, and European-culture conscious. Their connection with the Ivy League colleges rested on the fact that the large endowments of these institutions required constant consultation with the financiers of Wall Street.... As a consequence of these influences, as late as the 1930's, J. P. Morgan and his associates were the most significant figures in policy making at Harvard, Columbia, and to a lesser extent Yale, while the Whitneys were significant at Yale, and the Prudential Insurance Company (through Edward D. Duffield) dominated Princeton.

"The names of these Wall Street luminaries still adorn these Ivy League campuses, with Harkness colleges and a Payne Whitney gymnasium at Yale, a Payne dormitory at Princeton, a Dillon Field House and Lamont Library at Harvard. The chief officials of these universities were beholden to these financial powers and usually owed their jobs to them. Morgan himself helped make Nicholas Murray Butler president of Columbia; his chief Boston agent, Thomas Nelson Perkins of the First National Bank of that city, gave Conant his boost from the chemical laboratory to University Hall at Harvard; Duffield of Prudential, caught unprepared when the incumbent president of Princeton was killed in an automobile in 1932, made himself president for a year before he chose Harold Dodds for the post in 1933. At Yale, Thomas Lamont, managing partner of the Morgan firm, was able to swing Charles Seymour into the presidency of that university in 1937." (p. 937)

36

The Secret Network Included Prominent New York Law Firms:

"Closely allied with this Morgan influence were a small group of Wall Street Law firms, whose chief figures were Elihu Root, John W. Davis, Paul D. Cravath, Russell Leffingwell, the Dulles brothers and more recently, Arthur H. Dean, Philip D. Reed, and John J. McCloy. Other non-legal agents of Morgan included men like Owen D. Young and Norman H. Davis." (p. 952)

Beginning Of the Network's Power-structure In the American Press:

"The American Branch of this 'English Establishment' exerted much of its influence through five American newspapers. (*The New York Times,* New York *Herald Tribune, Christian Science Monitor,* the *Washington Post,* and the lamented *Boston Evening Transcript*). In fact, the editor of the *Christian Science Monitor* was the chief American correspondent (anonymously) of *The Round Table,* and Lord Lothian, the original editor of *The Round Table* and later secretary of the Rhodes trust (1925-1939) and ambassador to Washington, was a frequent writer in the Monitor." (p 953)

How the Anglo-American Secret Society Penetrated All Levels Of British and American Society:

"On this basis . . . there grew up in the twentieth century a power structure between London and New York which penetrated deeply into university life, the press, and the practice of foreign policy. In England the center was the Round Table Group, while in the United States it was J. P. Morgan and Company or its local Branches in Boston, Philadelphia, and Cleveland. Some rather incidental examples of the operations of this structure are very revealing, just because they are incidental. For example, it set up in Princeton a reasonable copy of the Round Table Group's chief Oxford headquarters, All Souls College. This copy, called the Institute for Advanced Study, and best known, perhaps, as the refuge of Einstein, Oppenheimer, John von Neumann, and George F. Kennan, was organized by Abraham Flexner of the Carnegie Foundation and Rockefeller's General Education Board after he had experienced the delights of All Souls while serving as Rhodes Memorial Lecturer at Oxford. The plans were largely drawn by Tom Jones, one of the Round Table's most active intriguers and foundation administrators. . . . It might be mentioned that the existence of this Wall Street, Anglo-American axis is quite obvious once it is pointed out. It is reflected in the fact that such Wall Street luminaries as John W. Davis, Lewis Douglas, Jock Whitney, and Douglas Dillon were appointed to be American ambassadors in London." (p.953)

HOW THE SECRET SOCIETY FORMED A COALITION
WITH THE COMMUNIST-SOCIALIST CONSPIRACY GROUPS

Dr. Quigley bluntly confesses that the International Bankers who had set out to remake the world were perfectly confident that they could use their money to acquire the cooperation and eventual control of the Communist-Socialist conspiratorial groups. In fact, John Ruskin of Oxford had persuaded the original Rhodes-Milner Round Table Groups that the way to federate the world was along socialistic lines, i.e., by having all property, industry, agriculture, communications, transportation, education and political affairs in the hands of a small cadre of financially-controlled political leaders who would organize the world and its peoples in a way which would compel everyone to do what was good for the new, world-society.

It may seem somewhat contradictory that the very people whom Marx identified as the epitome of "Capitalism" should be conspiring with the followers of Marx to overthrow traditional Capitalism and replace it with Socialism. But the record supports the Quigley contention that this is precisely what has been happening. The reason is rather simple.

Power from any source tends to create an appetite for additional power. Power coming from wealth tends to create an appetite for political power and visa versa. It was almost inevitable that the super-rich would one day aspire to control not only their own wealth, but the wealth of the whole world. To achieve this, they were perfectly willing to feed the ambitions of the power-hungry political conspirators who were committed to the overthrow of all existing governments and the establishments of a central world-wide dictatorship along socialist lines.

This, of course, was a risky business for the Anglo-American secret society. The super-rich were gambling on the expectation that when the violence and reconstruction had been completed by the political conspirators, the super-rich would then take over (like Plato's philosopher-kings, or ruling class), to guide mankind hopefully and compulsively into a whole new era of universal peace and universal prosperity.

To take such a risk, the cadre of the super-rich had to ignore the most elementary aspects of the ferocity of the left-wing conspiratorial mentality. Mao Tse-tung has articulated the basic Communist conviction that political power comes from the barrel of a gun and once they seize control it is their expressed intention to use the gun to prevent the super-rich or anyone else from taking that control away from them.

Nevertheless, the secret society of the London-Wall Street axis elected to take this risk. The master-planners have attempted to control the global conspiratorial groups by feeding them vast quantities of money for their revolutionary work and then financing their opposition if they seemed to be getting out of control. This policy has required the leaders of London and Wall Street to deliberately align themselves with dictatorial forces which have committed crimes against humanity in volume and severity unprecedented in history. It has required them to finance and support international intrigue by the most ruthless kind of political psychopaths. Studies show that many of these totalitarian political demogogues never would have come to power without the financial support of the super-rich. Studies further show that in many countries where the conspirators have taken over, the people would have risen up and overthrown them years ago if it had not been for the most sinister kind of depraved maneuvering behind the scenes by the agents of these wealthy master planners.

But for all this, Dr. Quigley pleads that these London-Wall Street manipulators had the best of intentions and were really angels in disguise. Here is the way he says it:

"The chief aims of this elaborate, semi-secret organization were largely commendable: to coordinate the international activities and outlooks of the English-speaking world into one (which would largely, it is true, be that of the London group); to work to maintain peace; to help backward, colonial, and underdeveloped areas to advance toward stability, law and order, and prosperity ALONG LINES SOMEWHAT SIMILAR TO THOSE TAUGHT AT OXFORD AND THE UNIVERSITY OF LONDON (ESPECIALLY THE SCHOOL OF ECONOMICS AND THE SCHOOLS OF AFRICAN AND ORIENTAL STUDIES)." (p. 954)

In this quotation emphasis is added so the reader will not miss Dr. Quigley's admission that the remaking of the world by the super-rich was to be along the socialist lines taught at those British institutions which look upon global Socialism as the hope of the world.

Dr. Quigley then continues his defense of these men whose record has been growing blacker with each Congressional investigation:

39

"These organizations and their financial backers were in no sense reactionary or Fascistic persons, as Communist propaganda would like to depict them. Quite the contrary. They were gracious and cultured gentlemen of somewhat limited social experience who were much concerned with the freedom of expression of minorities and the rule of law for all, who constantly thought in terms of Anglo-American solidarity, of political partition and federation, and who were convinced that they could gracefully civilize the Boers of South Africa, the Irish, the Arabs, and the Hindus, and who are largely responsible for the partitions of Ireland, Palestine, and India, as well as the federations of South Africa, Central Africa, and the West Indies. Their desire to win over the opposition by cooperation worked with Smuts but failed with Hertzog, worked with Gandhi but failed with Menon, worked with Stresemann but failed with Hitler, and has shown little chance of working with any Soviet leader. If their failures now loom larger than their successes, this should not be allowed to conceal the high motives with which they attempted both." (p. 954)

Having covered up the sins of his comrades-in-arms with the cloak of good intentions, Dr. Quigley returns to his role of historian:

How the Secret Society Became the Main Support For the Communists:

"It was this group of people, whose wealth and influence so exceeded their experience and understanding, who provided much of the framework of influence which the Communist sympathizers and fellow travelers took over in the United States in the 1930's. IT MUST BE RECOGNIZED THAT THE POWER THAT THESE ENERGETIC LEFT-WINGERS EXERCISED WAS NEVER THEIR OWN POWER OR COMMUNIST POWER BUT WAS ULTIMATELY THE POWER OF THE INTERNATIONAL FINANCIAL COTERIE. ..." (p. 954, emphasis added)

Of course, members of the dynastic banking families had been financing the Russian-oriented revolutionists for many years. Trotsky, in his biography, refers to some of these loans from British financiers going back as far as 1907. By 1917 the major subsidies for the revolution were being arranged by Sir George Buchanan and Lord Alfred Milner (of the Morgan-Rothschild-Rhodes confederacy). Milner, it will be recalled, was the founder of England's secret "Round Table" group which started the Royal Institute for International Affairs in England and the Council on Foreign Relations in the United States. One American source gave Trotsky, Lenin and the other Communist leaders around twenty million dollars for the final triumph of Bolshevism in Russia. This was Jacob Schiff of Kuhn, Loeb and

Company. The figure of twenty million dollars is cited by his grandson, Jacob Schiff, in the *New York Journal-American* for February 3, 1949. Other international bankers involved in the financing of the Communist take-over of Russia were Olaf Aschberg of the Nye Banken of Stockholm, the Rhine Westphalian Syndicate, and a wealthy banker named Jivotovsky whose daughter later married Leon Trotsky. However, the chief European funding came from Max Warburg of Germany whose two brothers, Felix and Paul Warburg, had moved to New York. Felix Warburg had become Jacob Schiff's son-in-law and Paul Warburg became Solomon Loeb's son-in-law. They both became partners in the Kuhn, Loeb and Company. (Paul Warburg, it will be recalled, had also been the principal promoter of the Federal Reserve System in the United States.) Between the Warburgs and Schiffs the money flowing to the Communist revolutionaries must have been substantial. Between 1918 and 1922 Lenin is supposed to have sent more than 600 million rubles in gold to Kuhn, Loeb and Company, Schiff's firm. (For additional details see *Czarism and the Revolution* by Arsene de Goulevitch and also *Western Technology and Soviet Economic Development—1917-1930* by Anthony C. Sutton, Hoover Institute, Stanford University, 1968.)

How the American Branch Of the Secret Society Barely Escaped Being Exposed:

". . . once the anger and suspicions of the American people were aroused, as they were by 1950, it was a fairly simple matter to get rid of the Red sympathizers. [Congressional committee reports show that they didn't get rid of them at all. The master planners just reshuffled and reassigned them. As soon as the Supreme Court had made shambles of the U. S. internal security laws, the hard-core came out of the woodwork again—WCS]. Before this could be done, however, a congressional committee, following backward to their source the threads which led from admitted Communists like Whitaker Chambers, through Alger Hiss, and the Carnegie Endowment to Thomas Lamont and the Morgan Bank, fell into the whole complicated network of the interlocking tax-exempt foundations. The Eighty-Third Congress in July 1953 set up a Special Committee to investigate Tax-Exempt Foundations with Representative B. Carroll Reece, of Tennessee, as chairman. It soon became clear that people of immense wealth would be unhappy if the investigation went too far and that the 'most respected' newspapers in the country, closely allied with these men of wealth, would not get excited enough about any revelations to make the publicity worthwhile,

41

in terms of votes or campaign contributions. An interesting report showing the Left-wing associations of the interlocking nexus of tax-exempt foundations was issued in 1954 rather quietly. Four years later, the Reece Committee's general counsel, Rene A. Wormser, wrote a shocked, but not shocking book on the subject called *Foundations: Their Power and Influence."* (pp. 954-955)

Rationale Behind the Support Of Communism:

"More than fifty years ago the Morgan firm decided to infiltrate the Left-wing political movements in the United States. This was relatively easy to do, since these groups were starved for funds and eager for a voice to reach the people. Wall Street supplied both. The purpose was not to destroy, dominate, or take over but was really threefold: (1) to keep informed about the thinking of Left-wing or liberal groups; (2) to provide them with a mouthpiece so that they could 'blow off steam,' and (3) to have a final veto on their publicity and possibly on their actions, if they ever went 'radical.' There was nothing really new about this decision, since other financiers had talked about it and even attempted it earlier." (p. 938)

"To Morgan all political parties were simply organizations to be used, and the firm always was careful to keep a foot in all camps. Morgan himself, Dwight Morrow, and other partners were allied with the Republicans; Russell C. Leffingwell was allied with the Democrats; Grayson Murphy was allied with the extreme Right; and Thomas W. Lamont was allied with the Left. Like the Morgan interest in libraries, museums, and art, its inability to distinguish between loyalty to the United States and loyalty to England, its recognition of the need for social work among the poor, the multipartisan political views of the Morgan firm in domestic politics went back to the original founder of the firm, George Peabody (1795-1869). To this same seminal figure may be attributed the use of tax-exempt foundations for controlling these activities, as may be observed in many part of America to this day, in the use of Peabody foundations to support Peabody libraries and museums. Unfortunately, we do not have space here for this great and untold story, but it must be remembered that what we do say is part of a much larger picture." (p. 945)

Lamont Represented Morgan In Various Communist Projects:

"Our concern at the moment is with the links between Wall Street and the Left, especially the Communists. Here the chief link was the Thomas W. Lamont family. This family was in many ways parallel to the Straight family. Tom Lamont had been brought into the Morgan firm, as Straight was several years later, by Henry P. Davison, a Morgan partner from 1909. Lamont became a partner in 1910, as Straight did in 1913. Each had a wife who became a patroness of Leftish causes, and two sons, of which the elder was a conventional banker, and the younger was a Left-wing sympathizer and sponsor. In fact, all the evidence would indicate that Tom Lamont was simply Morgan's apostle to the Left in succession to Straight, a change made necessary by the latter's premature death in 1918. Both were financial supporters of liberal publications, in Lamont's case *The Saturday Review of Literature,* which he supported throughout the 1920's and 1930's and the *New York Post,* which he owned from 1918 to 1924." (p. 945)

The Lamonts Helped Set Up Communist Front Organizations:

"The chief evidence, however, can be found in the files of the HUAC [House Un-American Activities Committee] which show Tom Lamont, his wife Flora, and his son Corliss as sponsors and financial angels to almost a score of extreme Left organizations, including the Communist Party itself. Among these we need mention only two. One of these was a Communist-front organization, the Trade Union Services, Incorporated, of New York City, which in 1947 published fifteen trade-union papers for various CIO unions. Among its officers were Corliss Lamont and Frederick Vanderbilt Field (another link between Wall Street and the Communists). The latter was on the editorial boards of the official Communist newspaper in New York, the *Daily Worker,* as well as its magazine, *The New Masses,* and was the Chief link between the Communists and the Institute of Pacific Relations in 1929-1947. Corliss Lamont was the leading light in another Communist organization which started life in the 1920's as the Friends of the Soviet Union, but in 1943 was reorganized, with Lamont as chairman of the board and chief incorporator, as the National Council of American-Soviet Friendship." (pp. 945-946)

The Lamonts Defied the U. S. Government In Its Attempt to Expose Their Operations:

"During this whole period of over two decades, Corliss Lamont [Tom Lamont's son], with the full support of his parents, was one of the chief figures in 'fellow traveler' circles and one of the chief spokesmen for the Soviet point of view both in these organizations and also in connections which came to him either as son of the most influential man in Wall Street or as professor of philosophy at Columbia

University. . . . In Januray, 1946, Corliss Lamont was called before HUAC to give testimony on the National Council of American-Soviet Friendship. He refused to produce records, was subpoenaed, refused, was charged with contempt of Congress, and was so cited by the House of Representatives on June 26, 1946. . . . The adverse publicity continued, yet when Thomas Lamont rewrote his will, on January 6, 1948, Corliss Lamont remained in it as co-heir to his father's fortune of scores of millions of dollars." (p. 946)

Morgan-Rockefeller-Carnegie Foundations Operated Through the IPR to Push China Into the Communist Camp:

"In 1951 the Subcommittee on Internal Security of the Senate Judiciary Committee, the so-called McCarran Committee, sought to show that China had been lost to the Communists by the deliberate actions of a group of academic experts on the Far East and Communist fellow travelers whose work in that direction was controlled and coordinated by the Institute of Pacific Relations (IPR). THE IN-FLUENCE OF THE COMMUNISTS IN IPR IS WELL ESTABLISHED, BUT THE PATRONAGE OF WALL STREET IS LESS WELL KNOWN.

"The IPR was a private association of ten independent national councils in ten countries concerned with affairs in the Pacific. The headquarters of the IPR and the American Council of IPR were both in New York and were closely associated on an interlocking basis. Each spent about $2.5 million dollars over the quarter-century from 1925 to 1950 of which about half, in each case, came from the Carnegie Foundation and the Rockefeller Foundation (which were themselves interlocking groups controlled by an alliance of Morgan and Rockefeller interests on Wall Street). Much of the rest [of the money], especially of the American Council, came from firms closely allied to these two Wall Street interests, such as Standard Oil, International Telephone and Telegraph, International General Electric, the National City Bank, and the Chase National Bank. . . .

"The financial deficits which occurred each year were picked up by financial angels, almost all with close Wall Street connections. The chief identifiable contributions here were about $60,000 from Frederick Vanderbilt Field over eighteen years, $14,700 from Thomas Lamont over fourteen years, $800 from Corliss Lamont (only after 1947) and $18,000 from a member of Lee, Higginson in Boston who seems to have been Jerome D. Greene." (pp. 946-947, emphasis added)

How the IPR Acquired Control Of U. S. Policies In the Far East:

"In addition, large sums of money each year were directed to private individuals, for research and travel expenses from similar sources, chiefly the great financial foundations.

"Most of these awards for work in the Far Eastern area required approval or recommendation from members of IPR. Moreover, access to publication and recommendations to academic positions in the handful of great American universities concerned with the Far East required similar sponsorship. And, finally, there can be little doubt that consultant jobs on Far Eastern matters in the State Department or other government agencies were largely restricted to IPR-approved people. The individuals who published, who had money, found jobs, were consulted, and who were appointed intermittently to government missions were those who were tolerant of the IPR line. The fact that all these lines of communication passed through the Ivy League universities or their scattered equivalents west of the Appalachians, such as Chicago, Stanford, or California, unquestionably went back to Morgan's influence in handling large academic endowments." (p. 947)

Dr. Quigley Admits the Facts But Tries to Obscure the Devastating Consequences of Outright Betrayal:

"There can be little doubt that the more active academic members of the IPR, the professors and publicists who became members of its governing board (such as Owen Lattimore, Joseph P. Chamberlain, and Philip C. Jessup of Columbia, William W. Lockwood of Princeton, John K. Fairbanks of Harvard, and others) and the administrative staff (which became, in time, the most significant influence in its policies) developed an IPR party line. It is, furthermore, fairly clear that this IPR line had many points in common both with the Kremlin's party line on the Far East and with the State Department's policy line in the same area. The interrelations among these, or the influence of one on another, is highly disputed. Certainly no conclusions can be drawn. Clearly there were some Communists, even party members, involved (such as Frederick Vanderbilt Field), but it is much less clear that there was any disloyalty to the United States. Furthermore, there was a great deal of intrigue both to help those who agreed with the IPR line and to influence United States government policy in this direction. BUT THERE IS NO EVIDENCE OF WHICH I AM AWARE OF ANY EXPLICIT PLOT OR CONSPIRACY TO DIRECT AMERICAN POLICY IN A DIRECTION FAVORABLE EITHER TO THE SOVIET UNION OR TO INTERNATIONAL COMMUNISM. Efforts of the radical Right to support their convictions about these last points undoubtedly did great, lasting, and unfair damage to the reputations and interests of many people." (pp. 947-948, emphasis added)

WHAT DID GOVERNMENT INVESTIGATIONS REVEAL CONCERNING IPR?

Dr. Quigley's shift of hats from historian to apologist pops up frequently throughout his 1,300-page volume, but nowhere is it more vividly evident than in the passage just quoted.

In this passage Dr. Quigley has tried to present the IPR party line, the State Department party line and the Soviet party line as three separate entities which just happened to coincide on the China issue. But barely ten pages earlier Dr. Quigley had been boasting how the IPR, a Soviet agent like Alger Hiss and top managers of the U. S. State Department were all interlocked through the London-Wall Street global control groups. He wrote: "Dean Rusk, Secretary of State after 1961, formerly president of the Rockefeller Foundation and Rhodes Scholar at Oxford (1931-1933), is as much a member of this nexus as Alger Hiss, the Dulles brothers, Jerome Greene, James T. Shotwell, John W. Davis, Elihu Root, or Philip Jessup." (p. 938)

And what was the "party line" the members of this "nexus" had evolved which just happened to coincide with that of the Soviet Union? It was simply that 600,000,000 Chinese should be turned over to the Communist bloc after the U. S. had fought the Japanese to keep them free. It was not the "radical right" who damaged the reputation of these particular gentlemen by exposing their "nexus" of IPR-State Department-Soviet intrigue, but the findings of the United States Congress and the investigations of IPR by the FBI. For example, toward the close of World War II, the office of the *Amerasia* magazine published by IPR was ordered investigated by the Attorney General. June 6, 1945, FBI agents searched the *Amerasia* headquarters and found over 1,800 top-secret documents which had been stolen from government files. Dr. Quigley claimed that he could find no evidence that IPR had engaged in any "plot or conspiracy to direct American policy in a direction favorable either to the Soviet Union or to International Communism." To reach such a conclusion he had to completely ignore the findings of fact by the bi-partisan Congressional committee which were as follows:

"During the period 1945-1949, persons associated with the Institute of Pacific Relations were instrumental in keeping United States policy on a course favorable to Communist objectives in China.

Persons associated with the IPR were influential in 1949 in giving United States far eastern policy a direction that furthered Communist purposes." (*Reece Committee Report,* Summary of Findings)

The Reece report listed whole columns of IPR members involved in Soviet intrigue, many of them officers of the U. S. State Department.

Dr. Quigley asks us to believe that even though there were "some Communists, even party members involved" in IPR, "it is much less clear that there was any disloyalty to the United States." (p.948)

Here is what the Reece Committee found:

"The IPR has been considered by the American Communist Party and by Soviet officials as an instrument of Communist policy, propaganda and military intelligence. The IPR disseminated and sought to popularize false information including information originating from Soviet and Communist sources. . . .

"Owen Lattimore was, from some time beginning in the 1930's, a conscious articulate instrument of the Soviet conspiracy. Effective leadership by the end of 1934 established and implemented an official connection with G. N. Voitinski, Chief of the Far Eastern Division of the Communist International. . . .

"The net effect of IPR activities on United States public opinion has been such as to serve internal Communist interests and to affect adversely the interests of the United States."

Not to mention the interests of 600,000,000 Chinese!

One of the singular and amazing things about Dr. Quigley's book is his willingness to frankly and unashamedly confess some of the most serious acts of subversion by his comrades-in-arms and then think nothing of turning around and flatly denying that they would have had a hand in such a foul and dirty business as betraying people like the Chinese to Communism.

We have observed above how shrewdly Dr. Quigley tried to obscure the catastrophic consequences of the betrayal of the Chinese, and yet, just over twenty pages earlier he had admitted:

"There is considerable truth in the [Nationalist] China Lobby's contention that the American experts on China were organized into a single interlocking group which had a general consensus of a Leftish character. It is also true that this group, from its control of funds, academic recommendations, and research or publication opportunities, could favor persons who accepted the established consensus and could injure, financially or in professional advancement, persons who did not accept it. It is also true that the established group, by its influence on book reviewing in *The New York Times,* the *Herald Tribune,* the *Saturday Review,* a few magazines, including the 'liberal weeklies,' and in the professional journals, could advance or hamper any specialist's career. It is also true that these things were done in the United States in regard to the Far East by the INSTITUTE OF PACIFIC RELATIONS, THAT THIS ORGANIZATION HAD BEEN INFILTRATED BY COMMUNISTS, AND BY COMMUNIST SYMPATHIZERS, AND THAT MUCH OF THIS GROUP'S INFLUENCE AROSE FROM ITS ACCESS TO AND CONTROL OVER THE FLOW OF FUNDS FROM FINANCIAL FOUNDATIONS TO SCHOLARLY ACTIVITIES." (p. 935, emphasis added)

In just a moment we will take a look at some of these secret, behind-the-scenes manipulators who poured millions of dollars into pro-Communist, pro-Socialist subversion of the United States and her allies.

DR. QUIGLEY SAYS ANTI-COMMUNISTS SHOOT BELOW THE REAL TARGET

Throughout his book, Dr. Quigley ridicules the stupid "Radical Right" (his favorite epithet for ordinary Americans trying to preserve their Constitutional prerogatives) and says they are missing the real target when they blame all the subversion and chicanery on the Communists. (See, for example, p. 949) One would expect him to go ahead and flatly deny that any genuine conspiracy exists, but not Dr. Quigley.

His attack on the "Radical Right" is primarily because of their "ignorance" in failing to recognize the vast, secret network of master planners for whom the Communists are working, particularly in Europe and the United States. In this connection and as part of his "confessional," Dr. Quigley describes with obvious satisfaction the antics of a notorious behind-the-scenes operator named Jerome D. Greene.

How Jerome Greene Rose to Power in the London-New York Axis:

"One of the most interesting members of this Anglo-American power structure was Jerome D. Greene (1874-1959). Born in Japan of missionary parents, Greene graduated from Harvard's college and law school by 1899 and became secretary to Harvard's president and corporation in 1901-1910. This gave him contacts with Wall Street which made him general manager of the Rockefeller Institute (1910-

48

1912), assistant to John D. Rockefeller in philanthropic work for two years, then trustee to the Rockefeller Institute, to the Rockefeller Foundation, and to the Rockefeller General Education Board until 1939. For fifteen years (1917-1932) he was with the Boston investment banking firm of Lee, Higginson, and Company, most of the period as its chief officer, as well as with its London branch. As executive secretary of the American section of the Allied Maritime Transport Council, stationed in London in 1918, he lived in Toynbee Hall, the world's first settlement house, which had been founded by Alfred Milner and his friends in 1884. This brought him in contact with the Round Table Group in England, a contact which was strengthened in 1919 when he was secretary to the Reparations Commission at the Paris Peace Conference. Accordingly, on his return to the United States he was one of the early figures in the ESTABLISHMENT OF THE COUNCIL ON FOREIGN RELATIONS, which served as the NEW YORK BRANCH OF LIONEL CURTIS'S INSTITUTE OF INTERNATIONAL AFFAIRS." (p. 955, emphasis added)

Jerome Greene Is Identified As the Spider In the IPR Web:

"Greene is of much greater significance in indicating the real influence within the Institute of Pacific Relations than any Communists or fellow travelers. He wrote the constitution for the IPR in 1926, was for years the chief conduit for Wall Street funds and influence into the organization, was treasurer of the American Council for three years, and chairman for three more, as well as chairman of the International Council for four years.

"Jerome Greene is a symbol of much more than the Wall Street influence in the IPR. He is also a symbol of the relationship between the financial circles of London and those of the eastern United States which REFLECTS ONE OF THE MOST POWERFUL INFLUENCES IN TWENTIETH-CENTURY AMERICAN AND WORLD HISTORY. The two ends of this English-speaking axis have sometimes been called, perhaps facetiously, the English and American establishments. There is, however, a considerable degree of truth behind the joke, a truth which reflects a VERY REAL POWER STRUCTURE. IT IS THIS POWER STRUCTURE WHICH THE RADICAL RIGHT IN THE UNITED STATES HAS BEEN ATTACKING FOR YEARS IN THE BELIEF THAT THEY WERE ATTACKING THE COMMUNISTS. This is particularly true when these attacks are directed, as they so frequently are, at 'Harvard Socialism,' or at 'Left-wing newspapers' like *The New York Times*, and the *Washington Post*, or at foundations and their dependent establishments, such as the Institute of International Education." (p. 956, emphasis added)

There Is a Conspiracy Bigger Than the Communist Conspiracy:
"There does exist, and has existed for a generation, an international Anglophile network which OPERATES, TO SOME EXTENT, IN THE WAY THE RADICAL RIGHT BELIEVES THE COMMUNISTS ACT. In fact, this network which we may identify as THE ROUND TABLE GROUPS, has no aversion to cooperating with the Communists, or any other groups, and frequently does so. I know of the operations of this network because I have studied it for twenty years and was permitted for two years, in the early 1960's, to examine its papers and secret records. I HAVE NO AVERSION TO IT OR TO MOST OF ITS AIMS AND HAVE, FOR MUCH OF MY LIFE, BEEN CLOSE TO IT AND TO MANY OF ITS INSTRUMENTS." (p. 950, emphasis added. We have quoted this passage earlier, but repeat it here because it pertains most significantly to the subject we are discussing.)

THE COUNCIL ON FOREIGN RELATIONS

Now it is time to take a closer look at the actual conspiratorial machinery of the global network of secret power, particularly as it relates to the domestic and foreign policy of the United States. As we have already discovered, the Secret Society set up by Cecil Rhodes in conjunction with Rothschild, Morgan, Carnegie, Rockefeller, *et al.*, was directed by a small highly secret Round Table Group. This secret group then set up fronts for the purposes of carrying forward its conspiratorial schemes. The United States front was called the Council on Foreign Relations. As we pointed out earlier, this is the way Dr. Quigley says it came into being:

"At the end of the war of 1914, it became clear that the organization of this system [the Round Table Group] had to be greatly extended. Once again the task was entrusted to Lionel Curtis who established, in England and each dominion, a front organization to the existing local Round Table Group. This front organization, called the Royal Institute of International Affairs, had as its nucleus in each area the existing submerged Round Table Group. In New York it was known as THE COUNCIL ON FOREIGN RELATIONS, AND WAS A FRONT FOR J. P. MORGAN AND COMPANY in association with the very small American Round Table Group.

"The American organizers were dominated by the large number of

Morgan 'experts' including Lamont and Beer, who had gone to the Paris Peace Conference and there became close friends with the similar group of English 'experts' which had been recruited by the Milner group. In fact, the original plans for the Royal Institute of International Affairs and the Council on Foreign Relations were drawn up in Paris." (pp. 951-952, emphasis added)

Although the Council on Foreign Relations is not the secret **inner** circle, its front activities are kept as mysterious as they are powerful. Practically no publicity is tolerated. If the student searches the recent periodicals for articles on the CFR, he is likely to find nothing. However, a more or less "official" account of what the Council wanted on the record was published by the *Christian Science Monitor,* September 1, 1961. This paper, according to Dr. Quigley, is part of the CFR-related press and therefore the article might be considered an official presentation. Here is the way the article opens up:

"On the west side of fashionable Park Avenue at 68th Street [New York City] sit two handsome buildings across the way from each other. ONE IS THE SOVIET EMBASSY TO THE UNITED NA-TIONS. . . . Directly opposite on the southwest corner is THE COUNCIL ON FOREIGN RELATIONS–probably one of the most influential semi-public organizations in the field of foreign policy." (emphasis added)

The CFR headquarters building was a gift of the Rockefellers.

The article states that "Its roster. . . contains names distinguished in the field of diplomacy, government, business, finance, science, labor, journalism, law and education. What united so wide-ranging and disparate a membership is a PASSIONATE CONCERN FOR THE DIRECTION OF AMERICAN FOREIGN POLICY."

The CFR roster has a formal membership of 1,400 elite person-alities carefully selected for their usefulness from all of the nation's key professions. These are screened and trained for decision-making positions in the Federal Government. The article states, "Almost half of the Council members have been invited to assume official govern-ment positions or to act as consultants at one time or another."

One other article may be found in one of the older magazines concerning the CFR. In *Harper's* of July, 1958, will be found an article entitled, "School For Statesmen," by CFR member, Joseph Kraft. He describes the CFR in these terms: "It has been the seat of . . . basic government decisions, has set the context for many more, and has repeatedly served as a recruiting ground for ranking officials." In this article, Kraft makes the point that CFR trains its members in a specific line of strategy to be carried out as part of the team in Washington. What is this strategy?

Kraft points out that the chief architect for the formal creation of CFR was the network's White House aid to President Wilson, "Colonel" Edward Mandell House, who worked hand in glove with Jerome Greene. House admitted writing *Philip Dru: Administrator* which described the creation of an international grouping of powers and establishing "Socialism as dreamed by Karl Marx." Kraft states that the carefully selected cadre of CFR supporters brought in to help House were Walter Lippmann, John Foster Dulles, Allen Dulles and Christian Herter. These were all with House at the Paris Peace Conference and House was the host for the Round Table Groups, both English and American, when they met on May 19, 1919, in the Majestic Hotel, Paris, to organize the front organizations for various parts of the world, the CFR in the United States being one of the most important.

To gain some idea of the power and influence of the CFR in literally taking over the foreign policy of the U. S. State Department after the war, we have the following from the State Department Publication 2349, entitled, *Report to the President On the Results of the San Francisco Conference.* It is the official report of the U. S. Secretary of State, Edward R. Stettinius:

"With the outbreak of war in Europe it was clear that the United States would be confronted, after the war, with new and exceptional problems. . . . Accordingly, a committee on Post-War Problems was set up before the end of 1939 [two years before the U. S. entered the war!], AT THE SUGGESTIONS OF THE CFR. The Committee consisted of high officials of the Department of State [all but one of whom were CFR members]. It was assisted by a research staff, which in February, 1941, was organized into a division of Special Research [meaning that it went off the CFR payroll to the State Department payroll]." (emphasis added)

This is the group which created the basic structure of the United Nations and the post-war policies which lost free peoples to the Communist bloc at the average rate of one hundred million per year for the first seven years after the war.

There were 74 CFR members in the American delegation to the U. N. Conference at San Francisco in 1945. They included Alger Hiss (Communist spy), Harry Dexter White (Soviet Agent), Owen Lattimore

Charter Members of the CFR

CHRISTIAN HERTER (upper left) who became Secretary of State.

JOHN FOSTER DULLES (upper right) who became Secretary of State.

ALLEN DULLES (right) who became head of the Central Intelligence Agency.

NELSON ROCKEFELLER

(described by a Congressional committee as a "conscious, articulate instrument of the Soviet international conspiracy"), John J. McCloy (formerly head of the Rockefeller Chase-Manhattan Bank), Harold Stassen, Nelson Rockefeller, John Foster Dulles, Philip Jessup and Dean Acheson. These and 38 additional CFR members occupied nearly every significant decision-making spot in the American delegation to the San Francisco conference to set up the United Nations.

One of the top families in the Morgan-Rockefeller axis has been the Lamonts, who loomed large in CFR circles and represented leading Wall Street bankers in fostering pro-Soviet policies and leading out in "help-the-Soviets" propaganda. CFR-member Corliss Lamont was named by the House Committee on Un-American Activities as "probably the most persistent propagandist for the Soviet Union to be found anywhere in the United States."

The Lamonts and other elite CFR members are interlocked with other Wall Street-financed programs, such as the American Association for the United Nations, the Foreign Policy Association, the World Affairs Council, the Committee for Economic Development, Business Advisory Council, Commission on National Goals, American Assembly, National Planning Association and Americans for Democratic Action.

Internationally, the CFR is interlocked with the Bilderbergers, the Pugwash Conferences, the English-speaking Union, the Pilgrims Society, and with its secret control-group, the Round Table.

The CFR has participated to some degree in each of the last **ten** administrations and dominated those of FDR, Truman, Eisenhower, (Eisenhower was the Establishment candidate against Taft), Kennedy, Johnson and the present administration as well. To illustrate the extent of CFR power in Washington at the present time, consider some of

54

these important CFR appointments made by President Nixon:

Henry A. Kissinger, Chief Foreign Policy Advisor. (coming directly from the paid staff of CFR)

Henry Cabot Lodge, Chief Negotiator in Paris.

Charles Yost, Ambassador to the United Nations. (also a paid staff member of the CFR)

Arthur Burns, Chairman of the Federal Reserve Board.

Harlan Cleveland, U. S. Ambassador to NATO.

George Ball, Foreign Policy Consultant.

Robert Murphy, special consultant on international affairs.

Richard P. Pederson, Exec. Sec., State Department.

Alan Pifer, consultant to the President on Educational Finance.

HENRY CABOT LODGE

Dr. Paul McCracken, chief economic aid.

Ellsworth Bunker, U. S. Ambassador to Saigon.

General Andrew J. Goodpaster, chief military policy advisor.

Dr. Glenn T. Seaborg, Chairman, Atomic Energy Commission.

Joseph J. Sisco, Assistant Secretary of State for the Middle East and South Asia.

Jacob Beam, Ambassador to the Soviet Union.

Gerald Smith, Director of the Arms Control and Disarmament Agency.

To further illustrate how thoroughly the policy-making operations of the White House have become integrated with those of the CFR, we have the perfectly frank admission by the Nixon administration that as of September 7, 1970, a brigadier general, Robert G. Gard, Jr., from the office of the Assistant Chief of Staff for Force Development, will be assigned to the headquarters of the Council on Foreign Relations

PRES. RICHARD NIXON

in New York City. (*Review of the News,* September 9, 1970, p. 17)

Every citizen who voted for Richard Nixon, including this reviewer, hoped that to some degree, at least, the new President would resist the collectivist Left and start the country back in the direction of common sense and the Constitution. On some fronts this has been done, but on many other fronts (in fact, on the most sensitive and decisive ones) the collectivist process has continued at an accelerated speed. Never has the bureaucratic staff at the White House been so large. Never have so many billions been requested for Federal subsidies to the states (with Federal control following closely on the heels of Federal money). These policies and programs are precisely what the obscure bosses behind the CFR have been urging for years. Another of their pet projects has been the recognition of Red China. There is already a definite softening by the Nixon Administration in that direction.

These facts are mentioned simply to alert the reader to the fact that Dr. Quigley may be entirely correct in his charge that the CFR and the Global Establishment have gained such a hold on the elective process in the United States that no matter which political party goes into power, the winner is beholden to those powers to a significant degree.

Of course, Mr. Nixon's opponent in the last election was one of the Global Establishment's most devoted disciples. Hubert Humphrey was a founder and the first vice-chairman of the Establishment's socialist-oriented ADA (Americans for Democratic Action), so if he had been elected instead of Mr. Nixon the pace of deterioration undoubtedly would have been even more massive and devastating.

The tragedy in all of this is the simple fact that the average tax-paying American was not given an honest and genuine choice. The voter finds himself enduring one party long enough to witness a whole series of travesties and then switches to the other party thinking he will get a substantial reversal of policy. But he doesn't. At best, all he gets is a slowing down in the collectivization process and in some areas it becomes even worse than it was before.

This situation is likely to continue until a sufficient number of Americans become angrily aroused and rise from the grass roots to seize control of one or both of the major political parties. Then the people can have a choice. Meanwhile, as the known facts now dramatically illustrate, the American electoral process is being manipulated by the Global Establishment precisely the way Dr. Quigley boasts that it is. At the end of this review we will discuss the steps which must be taken to liberate the American people from this colossal political trap.

TAX-EXEMPT FOUNDATIONS INVOLVED IN WEAKENING AND SUBVERTING THE CONSTITUTIONAL AND IDEOLOGICAL FABRIC OF THE AMERICAN CULTURE

Now we turn to the vast reservoirs of wealth—the tax-exempt foundations—which Dr. Quigley describes as the major base of operations for the Establishment bosses as they launch their catastrophic attack on the basic framework of the whole American society.

Dr. Quigley's disclosure that the Council on Foreign Relations and the Institute of Pacific Relations were responsible for what turned out to be a paroxysm of world-wide political subversion, is no more shocking than his bold declaration that the global collectivists of the London-Wall Street axis were equally successful in attacking the whole foundation of the American culture through the exploitation of the millions made available by certain tax-exempt foundations.

Generally speaking, the Rockefeller Foundation, the Carnegie Foundation, the Ford Foundation and a host of other Wall Street philanthropies have always been looked upon as generous, capitalistic santa clauses. Let us repeat a previous quotation in which Dr. Quigley admits the development of an explosive situation back in the early 1950's when the use of tax-exempt foundations for U. S. subversion ALMOST spilled out into public view. In fact, public hearings were heard, but the Establishment's choke-hold on the press was sufficient to keep the public from becoming aware of the scandalous proportions of the facts which were discovered. Here is the way Dr. Quigley describes what happened:

Tax-Exempt Foundations Caught Red-Handed:

"It must be recognized that the power that these energetic Left-wingers exercised was NEVER their own power nor Communist power but was ultimately THE POWER OF THE INTERNATIONAL FINANCIAL COTERIES, and, once the anger and suspicions of the American people were aroused, as they were by 1950, it was a fairly simple matter to GET RID OF [HIDE ELSEWHERE] THE RED SYMPATHIZERS. Before this could be done, however, a congressional committee, following backward to their source the THREADS WHICH LED FROM ADMITTED COMMUNISTS like Whittaker Chambers, through Alger Hiss, and the Carnegie Endowment to Thomas Lamont and the Morgan Bank, FELL INTO THE WHOLE COMPLICATED NETWORK OF INTERLOCKING TAX-EXEMPT FOUNDATIONS." (pp. 954-955, emphasis added)

How the Scandal Was Kept From Reaching the Public:

"The Eighty-third Congress in July 1953 set up a Special Committee to Investigate Tax-Exempt Foundations with Representative B. Carroll Reece, of Tennessee, as chairman. IT SOON BECAME CLEAR THAT PEOPLE OF IMMENSE WEALTH WOULD BE UNHAPPY IF THE INVESTIGATION WENT TOO FAR and that the 'most respected' newspapers in the country, CLOSELY ALLIED WITH THESE MEN OF WEALTH, would not get excited enough about any revelations to make the publicity worth while, in terms of votes or campaign contributions." (p. 955, emphasis added)

Note how this last sentence reveals the Achilles Heel in the secret society's operations. The whole concern of the globalist conspiracy is to do their work in such a way that the public will not become sufficiently aroused to use their "votes and campaign contributions" to knock the agents of the Establishment out of political power in Washington. As long as the Constitution remains in effect the American people still have an opportunity to wake up and "throw the rascals out." As we shall see later, Dr. Quigley was horrified, along with his fellow "insiders" when this earth-shaking possibility almost became a reality in 1964. But we shall discuss that tremendously interesting incident a little later. Now, back to Dr. Quigley:

The Scandalous Congressional Findings Were Not Shocking To Dr. Quigley:

"An interesting report SHOWING THE LEFT-WING ASSO-CIATIONS of the interlocking nexus of tax-exempt foundations was

58

issued in 1954 RATHER QUIETLY. Four years later, the Reece committee's general counsel, Rene A. Wormser, wrote a shocked, BUT NOT SHOCKING book on the subject called *Foundations: Their Power and Influence.*" (p. 955, emphasis added)

Note that Dr. Quigley fully appreciates that the Reece Committee hearings turned up some shocking information and that the book written by its general counsel, Rene A. Wormser, was intended to shock the public. But Dr. Quigley had been on the inside for many years so it was not shocking to him.

This reviewer has studied the Wormser book (Devin-Adair, New York, 1958) and has concluded that while the findings of the Reece Committee might not be disturbing to an "insider" like Dr. Quigley, they are certainly sufficient to raise the blood temperature of any ordinary American who might be anxious to preserve his basic rights and preserve the American way of life in an open society. The Reece Committee found that tax-exempt foundations were deliberately attacking the whole basic structure of the Constitution and the Judaic-Christian American culture.

A CONGRESSIONAL COMMITTEE VERIFIES WHAT DR. QUIGLEY SAYS CONCERNING THE POWER OF TAX-EXEMPT FOUNDATIONS

For the sake of brevity, the facts set forth in the Wormser book on the findings of the Reece Committee will be summarized. The various references to the specific pages where the details can be read are provided:

1. Political maneuvering to prevent the hearings from being effective. (pp. 341-377)
2. Completely disruptive tactics employed by Congressman Wayne Hays. (pp. 359-366)
3. How rich banking and industrial families give their money to foundations without losing control of their funds. (pp. 11-12)
4. Who actually runs the tax-exempt foundations? (pp. 41-54)
5. How the major foundations are all interlocked into a monolithic monopoly of power to carry out globalist policies. (pp. 57-80)
6. Money of the foundations used to take over the Social Sciences:
   a. Social Sciences looked upon as a potential political

59

instrument. (pp. 83-86)
b. Suppressing social scientists who disagree or criticize. (pp. 86-89)
c. Developing an elite corps of social engineers with a compulsive drive to "remake the world" along socialist lines. (pp. 90-100)
d. Foundation-sponsored Kinsey report deliberately designed as an attack on Judaic-Christian morality. (pp. 100-105)
e. Using social science to sabotage the structure of military services. (pp. 105-110)
f. Employing a Marxist Socialist to produce and promote the social science classic, "A Proper Study of Mankind." (pp. 110-114)
g. Importing a Swedish Socialist to produce a study on the American Negro which has created the current climate of revolution and violence. (pp. 114-119)
h. Financing *The Encyclopedia of the Social Sciences* as a vehicle for the spreading of socialist concepts. (pp. 119-125)
i. Developing a Marxist elite in academic social science circles. (pp. 125-129)
j. Policy of continually emphasizing pathological aspects of American society to discredit its culture. (pp. 129-131)
k. Foundation-sponsored research often slanted to conform with pre-conceived objectives. (pp. 75, 131-138)
7. Foundations use their funds to subvert and control American education.
a. "Conform or no grant!" (p. 140)
b. The birth of Educational Radicalism. (pp. 143-145)
c. Carnegie finances a Socialist charter for education. (pp. 146-152)
d. The radical educators. (pp. 152-155)
e. The Progressive Education Association. (pp. 155-156)
f. Financing and promoting socialist textbooks. (pp. 156-167)
g. Financing Left-wing reference works. (pp. 167-171)
h. The National Education Association not designed to advance "American" education. (pp. 142, 145, 160, 164-165, 216-217)
8. Tax-Exempt Foundations as instruments of subversion:
a. Communist influences in foundations. (pp. 174-177)
b. Socialist influences in foundations. (pp. 177-184)

60

c. Helplessness of the average citizen. (pp. 186-187)
d. Ridiculing the American idea of free markets and free enterprise. (pp. 187-188)
e. The Socialists receive voluminous foundation-support in launching their League for Industrial Democracy. (pp. 188-193)
f. Foundations push a long-range program to radicalize American labor. (pp. 193-196)
g. Foundations provide Communists, Socialists and similar collectivist mentalities to serve in government. (pp. 196-199)
9. Foundations finance the betrayal of America's best interest to achieve collectivist internationalism:
a. Foundation policies fixed on global schemes. (pp. 200-201)
b. Rhodes scholars fed into Government service by foundations. (pp. 201-202)
c. The Carnegie Endowment for International Peace caught promulgating war. (p. 204)
d. International Relations Clubs sponsored by Carnegie to promote socialist internationalism and speakers such as Alger Hiss. (pp. 207-208)
e. The Foreign Policy Association as an instrument of opinion-molding to the Left. (pp. 208-209)
f. History books which keep Americans from learning the truth. (pp. 209-210)
g. Promoting the United Nations as the home base for the Socialist-Communist coalition. (pp. 214-216)
h. Alger Hiss describes how foundation agencies should be used to affect U. S. policy decisions. (pp. 218-219)

THE FORD FOUNDATION RECEIVES SPECIAL ATTENTION

The Wormser book devotes 79 pages exclusively to the Ford Foundation. Even in 1958 Wormser sensed that the newest and largest of the dynastic foundations was being harnessed to the team of global internationalism and that its guns were quick to blast away at any traditional Americans who were bold enough to suggest that the open society of the United States might be preferable to the great new society of controlled collectivism.

The irony of this tragic abuse of Ford Foundation funds was

61

HENRY FORD

compounded by the fact that Henry Ford, Sr., had maintained a running battle with the Wall Street tycoons to keep them from taking over his company during his latter years. He set up the Ford Foundation in such a way that his family would be able to keep control of it and he had assumed they would perpetuate the same policies and ideas which he had fostered. But when Henry Ford, Sr. died in 1947, there was a scramble for power and the chief responsibility for the actual administration of the Ford Foundation ended up in the hands of none other than Paul G. Hoffman.

Paul G. Hoffman was not only a member of the London-Wall Street nexus, but had been director of the principal propaganda arm of the COUNCIL ON FOREIGN RELATIONS and also a trustee for the INSTITUTE OF PACIFIC RE-LATIONS. Hoffman hired a well-known global collectivist, Robert M. Hutchins, as his $50,000 per year Associate Director. They were deeply involved in various Left-wing enterprises until 1953 when the Ford family went through a "palace revolution" and Hoffman and Hutchins found themselves being handed $15 million to set up a "Fund For the Republic" so they could be replaced on the Ford Foundation management team by more immediate friends of the family.

As the directors of the new Fund for the Republic, Hoffman and Hutchins immediately went to work suppressing in every way possible the strong spirit of anti-Communism which had exploded after the Hiss scandal and the frustrations of the Korean War. They spent $100,000 in a "study" of the Government's loyalty-security program and helped to completely emasculate the peace-time defenses against subversive employees in Government. They also spent $300,000 on a "study" of the "influence of Communism in contemporary America." A key member of the staff for this study was Earl Browder, long-time

National Secretary of the Communist Party. Another "study" tried to discredit the efforts of concerned citizens who were stirring up public opinion to keep known Communists from propagandizing on radio, television and the motion picture screen. When concerned parents began objecting to hard-core Left-wing teachers in the state schools and colleges, the Fund for the Republic spent $150,000 to demonstrate that academic freedom was being suppressed by "over-zealous patriots." When J. Robert Oppenheimer was fired as a security risk after he was found to have lied about his contributions to the Communist Party, the Fund for the Republic financed and promoted the showing of Edward R. Murrow's propaganda broadside defending Oppenheimer. When the American Friends Service Committee was trying to whitewash

PAUL HOFFMAN

the Communist seizure of China and get the United States to grant recognition, Hoffman went to the Ford Foundation and successfully obtained $1,134,000 to finance their campaign.

Hoffman soon depleted the $15 million given the Fund for the Republic, but he then married Mrs. Anna Rosenberg and took a key post at the United Nations where he helped get several millions in U. S. funds turned over in the name of the U. N. to Castro and otherwise supported a wide variety of Communist-sponsored projects.

Meanwhile Robert M. Hutchins had reorganized the Fund for the Republic and created a radical Left-wing propaganda organization in Santa Barbara, California, called the Center for the Study of Democratic Institutions. New financing had to be obtained, much of it through foundation grants. The activities of this Center became so notorious that the Ford Foundation would no longer admit whether or not it was providing additional financing.

By 1956 the Ford Foundation had spent more than one billion

ROBERT HUTCHINS

dollars in contributions to "education" and had thereby become a well-nigh all-encompassing influence over hundreds of colleges and universities.

McGEORGE BUNDY BECOMES PRESIDENT OF THE FORD FOUNDATION

By 1966 it was decided to place the Ford Foundation in the hands of McGeorge Bundy and many people—already concerned about the trend of this foundation's expenditures—were alarmed to see it suddenly make its major project the financing of the newly radicalized revolutionary Left.

Who is McGeorge Bundy?

After graduation from Yale, Bundy was employed on the staff of the COUNCIL ON FOREIGN RELATIONS. In a short time he launched on an academic career and succeeded in becoming the dean of the faculty of arts and sciences at Harvard by the age of 34. From there he was drafted to serve as a top advisor to John F. Kennedy and Lyndon Johnson. They placed him in the leadership of the highly sensitive National Security Council. In 1964 when the Communist elements tried to seize the Dominican Republic and U. S. forces had to be dispatched to prevent another Red Cuba from arising in the Caribbean, McGeorge Bundy was sent over to find a "political" solution. He selected Antonio Guzman, one of the top henchmen of the leader of the Communist coup as the man to support. Some alert Washington correspondent went to work and publicized the fact that Guzman was not only the official negotiator for the Communist-dominated Bosch regime, but was under investigation for a $75 million theft from the Banco Agricultura which Guzman had managed during the short time Bosch was in power. A storm of protest broke in Congress when it was discovered what McGeorge Bundy was trying to do. Bundy

64

returned quickly to Washington and was soon out of Government service. It was then announced that he was going to be the new President of the Ford Foundation.

(It was reminiscent of the handling of the Alger Hiss scandal. As the subversive career which Hiss had nurtured through the years began to be exposed, and embarrass the administration, he was quickly removed from his official assignment with the State Department and appointed President of the Carnegie Endowment for International Peace.)

McGeorge Bundy accepted his new assignment with the Ford Foundation as very serious business. He soon announced that the militant "Black Revolution" was "the first of the nation's problems." Bundy's solution was to pour vast quantities

McGEORGE BUNDY

of funds into the hands of the professional Black revolutionists.

In New York City one of the foremost firebrands in the violent racial riots which have plagued that metropolis, has been Milton A. Galamison. He was the keynote speaker at the organizing convention of the Communist W.E.B. Dubois Clubs. In 1967 Bundy authorized $160,000 to underwrite Galamison's revolutionary work.

A Black revolutionist, Herman B. Ferguson, identified himself with R.A.M., which turned out to be a Communist-front terror organization. In due time Ferguson was indicted in Queens, N.Y., on a charge of plotting the assassination of non-Communist Negro leaders and Senator Robert F. Kennedy. With such a serious charge pending against him, Ferguson was nevertheless hired by the Ford Foundation and he was still on the rolls of the Foundation when he was finally arrested for violating the terms of his bail.

LeRoi Jones made himself notorious as the author of a vulgar anti-white play called *The Toilet.* He was encouraged to go on with his revolutionary theatrical pornography when he was given access to

65

a grant of $50,000 from the Ford Foundation. Later, Jones was arrested in Newark, N. J. while helping to lead the 1967 riots at Newark. He was heavily armed.

The National Urban League whose chief is Whitney M. Young, started out as a moderate Negro public service agency. But when it came out against non-violence and in favor of Black Power, the League received approximately $2 million from the Ford Foundation.

Floyd B. McKissick, Stokely Carmichael's associate in the Black Power movement, obtained $175,000 from the Foundation for the anti-White racist organization, CORE. A year later (1968) the Ford Foundation gave CORE $300,000 more.

When Walter Reuther decided to "unionize" Welfare and O.E.O. recipients so they could bring greater pressure on Government to insure increased stipends, the Ford Foundation initiated the program (called the "Citizens Crusade Against Poverty") with a grant of $508,500. Reuther is the man who took a training job in the Soviet Union and wrote back to his friends, "Carry on the fight for a Soviet America."

Official Ford Foundation reports show that millions upon millions are being poured into revolutionary, Communist-dominated or global collectivist organizations under the direction of McGeorge Bundy. Here are a few samples from recent reports. Anyone familiar with the Congressional reports on Un-American Activities will appreciate the significance of these organizations.

COUNCIL ON FOREIGN RELATIONS ($1,000,000)

ADLAI E. STEVENSON INSTITUTE OF INTERNATIONAL AFFAIRS ($1,000,000)

INSTITUTE OF INTERNATIONAL EDUCATION ($1,625,000)

WORLD AFFAIRS COUNCIL ($102,000)

THE NATIONAL COMMITTEE ON U.S.-CHINA [Red China] RELATIONS ($250,000)

THE UNITED NATIONS ASSOCIATION ($150,000)

FOREIGN POLICY RESEARCH ($275,000)

AMERICAN FRIENDS SERVICE COMMITTEE [pro-Vietcong] ($100,000)

SOUTHERN REGIONAL COUNCIL [Communist staffed] ($648,000)

NATIONAL STUDENT ASSOCIATION ($315,000)

SOUTHWEST COUNCIL OF LA RAZA [headed by identified Communist Maclevie R. Barraza] ($630,000)

NATIONAL EDUCATION-
AL TELEVISION AND
RADIO CENTER [N.E.T.]
($6,000,000)
PUBLIC BROADCAST LAB-
ORATORY ($7,900,000)
So much for the activities of
the major foundations which "in-
sider" Carroll Quigley says were
"not shocking" to him at all.

DR. QUIGLEY'S ASSESSMENT OF CERTAIN PROMINENT PEOPLE ON THE U. S. SCENE

Dwight Eisenhower and Richard Nixon:

"The candidate [Eisenhower]
had no particular assets except a
bland and amiable disposition combined with his reputation as a
victorious general. He also had a
weakness, one which is frequently
found in his profession, the con-

PRES. DWIGHT D. EISENHOWER

viction that anyone who has become a millionaire, even by inheritance,
is an authoritative person on almost any subject. With Eisenhower as
candidate, combined with RICHARD NIXON, the ruthless enemy of
internal subversion, as a running mate, and using a campaign in which
the power of Madison Avenue publicity mobilized all the forces of
American discontent behind the neo-isolationist program, victory in
November, 1952, was assured." (p. 987, emphasis added)

". . . the lower-middle-class groups had preferred Senator Taft
as their leader. Eisenhower, however, had been preferred by the
EASTERN ESTABLISHMENT of old Wall Street, Ivy League, semi-
aristocratic Anglophiles whose real strength rested in their control of
eastern financial endowments, operating from foundations, academic
halls, and other tax-exempt refuges." (p. 1244, emphasis added)

John F. Kennedy:

"Kennedy, despite his Irish Catholicism, was an Establishment
figure. This did not arise from his semi-aristocratic attitudes or his

67

DEAN RUSK

Harvard connections. . . . These helped, but John Kennedy's introduction to the Establishment arose from his support of Britain, in opposition to his father, in the critical days at the American Embassy in London in 1938-1940. His acceptance into the English Establishment opened its American branch as well. The former was indicated by a number of events, such as sister Kathleen's marriage to the Marquis of Hartington and the shifting of Caroline's nursery school from the White House to the British Embassy after her father's assassination. (The ambassador, Ormsby-Gore, fifth Baron of Harlech, was the son of an old associate of Lord Milner and Leo Amery, when they were the active core of the British-American Atlantic Establishment.) Another indication of this connection was the large number of Oxford-trained men appointed to office by President Kennedy." (p. 1245)

Dean Rusk, Alger Hiss, John Foster Dulles, Etc.:

"These tax laws drove the great private fortunes dominated by Wall Street into tax-exempt foundations which became a major link in the Establishment network between Wall Street, the Ivy League, and the Federal Government. DEAN RUSK, Secretary of State after 1961, formerly president of the Rockefeller Foundation and Rhodes Scholar at Oxford (1931-1933) is as much a member of the nexus as ALGER HISS, the DULLES BROTHERS, JEROME GREENE, JAMES T. SHORTWELL, JOHN W. DAVIS, ELIHU ROOT, OR PHILIP JESSUP." (p. 938, emphasis added)

THE SUBVERSION OF AMERICAN EDUCATION

Beginning on page 980, Dr. Quigley mentions an incident which demonstrates how powerful tycoons of international finance have competed with each other behind the scenes to dominate American educational institutions. Speaking of Columbia University, Dr. Quigley says: "This, of all universities, had been the one closest to J. P. Morgan and Company, and its president, Nicholas Murray Butler, was Morgan's chief spokesman from ivied halls. He had been chosen under Morgan influence, but the events of 1930-1948 which so weakened Morgan in the economic system also weakened his influence on the board of trustees of Columbia, until it became evident that Morgan did not have the votes to elect a successor. However, Morgan (that is Tom Lamont) did have the votes to preserve the *status quo* and, accordingly, President Butler was kept in his position until he was long past his physical ability to carry on

PHILIP JESSUP

its functions. Finally, he had to retire. Even then Lamont and his allies were able to prevent choice of a successor, and postponed it, making the university treasurer acting-president, in the hope that a favorable change in the board of trustees might make it possible for Morgan, once again, to name a Columbia president.

"Fate decreed otherwise, for Lamont died in 1948, and shortly afterward, a committee of trustees under Thomas Watson of International Business Machines was empowered to seek a new president. This was not an area in which the genius of IBM was at his most effective. While on a business trip to Washington, he confided his problem to a friend who helpfully suggested, 'Have you thought of Eisenhower?' By this he meant Milton Eisenhower, then president of Penn State, later president of Johns Hopkins; Watson, who apparently did not think immediately of this lesser-known member of the Eisenhower family, thanked his friend, and began the steps which soon made Dwight Eisenhower, for two unhappy years, president of Columbia."

69

But it did not seem to matter which financial coterie behind the scenes appointed the President of Columbia; its policies followed the mainstream of world collectivism. Thus, Dwight Eisenhower vocally denounced the possibility that Columbia could be a hotbed of Communist intrigue (New York Star, August 18, 1948, p. 1) and then turned around and accepted an endowment from the Communist government of Poland to set up a "Chair of Polish Studies" and appointed the well-known Marxist, Dr. Manfred Kridl, to fill the position. It would be extremely interesting to know what forces worked on Dwight Eisenhower to get him to take this rather amazing step when even his own liberally-oriented faculty objected.

But some strange things had been going on for many years at Columbia. The father of Progressive Education, John Dewey, made Columbia his chief center of operations. His favorite students and disciples, William H. Kilpatrick, Harold O. Rugg and George S. Counts, also claimed Columbia's Teacher's College as their headquarters. These men had been preaching some strange doctrines for many years and were receiving millions in endowments for their efforts. As Dr. Felix Wittmer pointed out in his book, *Conquest of the American Mind,* "Have you ever read a book on 'curriculum development?' No one should blame you if you haven't. If you have, you may understand a little better what has happened to the schools in your community and how it has come about.

"As the years went by, and your children passed through the grades, you may have noticed that a change was going on. Subject matter, teaching methods, types of study, everything changed. If you put two and two together, you realized that the emphasis shifted from the individual to the group.

"Your children learned that the *Communist Manifesto* ranked among the great works of world literature, and that the Soviet Union was an 'economic democracy.' They laughingly approved of the increase in 'snap courses.' Competition, it seems, had become old hat. 'Attitudes' and 'group relationships' were the thing.

"Just who was responsible for the change you could not say. 'Trends of the times' hardly seems to be a penetrating explanation. Fact is that a relatively small group of educators, who gravitated toward Columbia Teachers College, have in the course of twenty years turned thousands and thousands of teachers into missionaries of the collectivist, i.e., socialist, creed. These thousands of converts have brought about the change." (Meador Publishing Co., Boston, 1956, p. 39)

What John Dewey and his disciples were teaching may be gleaned from any of their official publications. In *Democracy and the Curriculum,* Harold Rugg and George S. Counts said the open society of America was way behind the times. They called it a "continuously depressed society" and said it even contained the "seed of incipient facism." (p. 524) They denounced the Constitutional system of checks and balances as a "liability" and deplored the fact that the Constitution "is calculated to make the administration of the public welfare feeble, uncertain and inefficient" (p. 210). After making frequent pilgrimages to the Soviet Union the Columbia Teachers College missionaries would urge the hastening of America's adoption of a "managed economy."

As early as 1932, Dr. Counts had written his 56-page booklet entitled, *Dare the Schools Build a New Social Order?* In it he had demanded that education must free itself from the influence of the middle classes. He said "the teachers should deliberately reach for power and then make the most of their conquest." (p. 28) Of course, most teachers were not after power. They merely wanted to be left alone to teach school. Before long, however, they were getting policies from the National Educational Association and being required to teach from texts which contained some rather astonishing concepts. A genuine anti-Americanism began to appear in texts which downgraded traditional ideals and basic concepts of economics and government. Many books have analyzed this assault on the American culture in addition to Dr. Wittmer's *Conquest of the American Mind.* Dr. E. Merril Root has written two excellent books, *Brain Washing in the High Schools* (Devin Adair, 1959), and *Collectivism on the Campus* (Devin Adair, 1961). Augustin G. Rudd's *Bending of the Twig* also deals with the invasion of the American schools for subversive purposes.

These authors were able to document the fact that for many years American schools have been infiltrated with a steady stream of amorality, humanism, collectivism and anti-individualism emanating from Columbia's Teachers College, the National Education Association and other Establishment centers. These centers have served as launching pads to attack the political and economic structure of the American system.

And what has been the result?

Dr. Quigley frankly admits that it has been rather awful in many respects. Summing up at the end of his book, he says, "Some things we clearly do NOT know, including the most important of all, which is HOW TO BRING UP CHILDREN to form them into MATURE,

RESPONSIBLE ADULTS. . . ." (p. 1311, emphasis added)

This is a shocking admission. It is a confession of total incompetence in a field where parents know there IS a way to develop the vast majority of human beings into mature, responsible adults.

In fact, it is this precise conviction which leads American parents to pay billions in taxes for their children's education. Nevertheless, for many years both parents and teachers have sensed that strong, heavily financed left-wing influences have been doing their best to foster a climate of hedonistic nihilism among the schools. If these people had their way we would develop a prospective nightmare in our schools–schools without grades, without discipline, without prayers, without pledges of allegiance, without Christmas, without Easter, without patriotism, without morals, without standards of speech or standards of dress.

Already, wherever they have taken over the educational system, we see the worst of their products–intellectual guerrillas emerging from the universities trained in "participatory mobocracy."

Surely the nation deserves something better than this for the billions it is spending.

THE SLOW AWAKENING OF THE SLUMBERING GIANT

Off and on throughout the past fifty years there have been explosive moments when the action of the subversive conspiratorial coalition ALMOST aroused the American people to a conscious state of alertness and alarm.

Dr. Carroll Quigley admits that nothing panics the international Establishment like the possibility of a threatened exposure. (See, for example, p. 954.) Whenever the public has become dangerously aware of the conspiratorial processes operating around them, the vast, interlocking power structure of the whole London-Wall Street combine has immediately shifted into high gear and raced to the rescue. Radio, TV, newspapers, magazines, government policy makers, college officials, intellectual pundits and other opinion moulders in high places have all commenced a recitation of a carefully prepared "line" designed to pacify the public and put them back to sleep.

It is interesting to watch Dr. Quigley discuss a number of these Establishment crises. As he writes about those few occasions when the American people were beginning to awaken. Quigley tends to abandon

72

his role of historian and commences to engage in the most bitter kind of polemics against those people he calls the "middle class mentality" who had the audacity to sound the alarm and delay the Establishment's march toward a global society of socialized authoritarianism.

In the interest of brevity, we will only go back two or three decades to mention a few of the times when the American people ALMOST awakened sufficiently to blow the Establishment out into the bright white light of public scrutiny.

Anyone studying the Congressional hearings of the past 30 years will see how often there was an opportunity to turn the tide of history if ENOUGH Americans could have been awakened to insist upon it. Future historians will probably count it a tragedy that in each instance the Establishment was successful in soothing the public indignation so that little of their ground was lost.

Here are a few headlines from the past.

Harry Hopkins Gives Atomic Secrets and Uranium to Russia

Right after World War II, Major Racey Jordan, expeditor of Russian lend-lease, disclosed that his one-time boss, Harry Hopkins, had secretly secured the latest know-how on the atomic bomb as of 1943 and shipped it to Russia in a lend-lease plane which Jordan found to be loaded with black suitcases containing espionage files on the United States. When Jordan grounded this plane and flew to Washington to make an issue of this betrayal of U.S. interests he found himself threatened with severe disciplinary action. He was later ordered by Harry Hopkins to approve and ship to Russia (without making a record of it) several shipments of refined uranium compounds which experts later estimated to have been more than was necessary to produce an atomic explosion. The testimony of Major Jordan before a Congressional Committee is summarized in his book, *From Major Jordan's Diaries* (New York: Harcourt, Brace and Company, 1952).

Naturally, this scandal caused considerable excitement for awhile, but today few people even remember it. Harry Hopkins died shortly after the war so the matter was never pursued. In 1949 Russia exploded her first atomic bomb, years ahead of general expectations.

State Department Involved in Russian Take-Over of Eastern Europe

Within a short time after World War II, it began to become apparent that all of Eastern Europe was ending up under Soviet control and the promised freedom of those nations was being deliberately betrayed by certain Washington policy makers. These activities became

HARRY HOPKINS

so brazen that it caused Ambassador Arthur Bliss Lane to resign and write his shocking and authoritative book, *I Saw Poland Betrayed* (New York: Bobbe-Merrill Co., 1949). David Martin wrote how the same kind of tactics were used to betray the anti-Communist forces who fought to liberate Yugoslavia. Martin called his book, *Ally Betrayed* (New York: Prentice-Hall, 1946). Thus it went up and down the Eastern European corridor. What Hitler lost, Stalin gained.

It was very popular at that time for the Establishment's liberal press to join with liberal professors and Left-wing congressmen to assure the American people that these countries were merely going "Socialist" to solve their problems and this would prevent the Communists from taking over. The fraudulent and fallacious nature of this claim led to the complete disillusionment of a prominent Socialist in the British Parliament named Ivor Thomas. He wrote a book showing how the Socialists made it easy for the Communists to take over in Eastern Europe. It is called *The Socialist Tragedy* (New York: The Macmillan Company, 1951).

State Department Involved in the Communist Conquest of China

General Albert C. Wedemeyer was the last commander of the Chinese Theater of Operations during World War II, and he has described in his book, *Wedemeyer Reports* (New York: Henry Holt & Co., 1958), how he assured Chiang Kai-shek that the U.S. would support the Nationalist Chinese in setting up a democratic form of government after the war. But this never came about, because right at the time the delicate process of writing and adopting a constitution was in process, the State Department sent over George C. Marshall to tell Chiang Kai-shek that if he didn't allow the Communist Chinese to immediately enter his government on a coalition basis, all U.S. aid would be terminated. General Wedemeyer wrote a comprehensive report to President Truman showing how this fantastic demand would ultimately lead to a Communist conquest of 600,000,000 Chinese. The State Department demanded that General Wedemeyer be "muzzled." Chiang Kai-shek refused to accept the Communists in his government, and General Marshall fulfilled his threat. He wrote: "As Chief of Staff I armed 39 anti-Communist divisions (in China), now with a stroke of the pen I disarm them." U.S. aid to China was reduced to a dribble. Both economic and military collapse became inevitable.

GEORGE C. MARSHALL

We have already discussed the Establishment's manipulation of the State Department through its Institute of Pacific Relations, which set the stage for the betrayal of China to a Communist conquest.

By 1949 the whole mainland of China was in Communist hands and a bloodbath of genocidal terrorism was being poured out upon the people. What Americans had fought World War II to prevent the Japanese from doing to China, the State Department had encouraged Mao and Chao to go ahead and accomplish.

The next task was to keep the American people from discovering how China had been betrayed to the Reds. It was necessary to cover the tracks of the IPR and its agents who were working inside the U.S. government. Dean Acheson, Secretary of State, wrote a notorious *White Paper* trying to put the blame on Chiang Kai-shek and saying the State Department had been helpless to prevent the Communist coup. However, Acheson's ambassador to China, John Leighton Stuart, wrote a book called *Fifty Years in China* (New York: Random House, 1955) in which he admitted that he and his associates in the State Department could not escape their "part of the responsibility of the great catastrophe." He repudiated the *White Paper* as a historical document and said it left out much of what really happened. Professor Kenneth Colegrove of the Political Science Department at Northwestern University went even further. He said Dean Acheson's *White Paper* "was one of the most false documents ever published by any country." (*Institute of Pacific Relations Hearings,* Part 3, p. 923)

State Department Official, Alger Hiss, Exposed as Soviet Spy

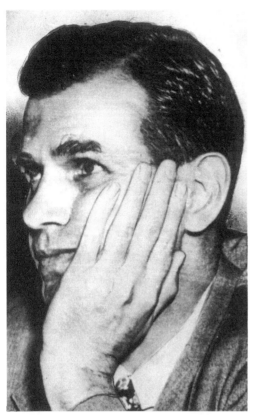

ALGER HISS

Even before World War II, President Roosevelt had been warned that Alger Hiss was a top spy of the Soviet Union. The information came from no less an authority than the chief courier of the Soviet Union in Washington, D. C., who was getting ready to defect. His name was Whittaker Chambers. Unfortunately, President Roosevelt refused to believe the story or even check on it, so Whittaker Chambers went underground and eventually became the senior editor of *Time* magazine. Not until 1948 did the full exposure take place before the House Committee on Un-American Activities. Hiss had meanwhile risen to become a top official of the State Department, a closely trusted advisor to the President, and had been made the key-administrator in setting up the United Nations. As of 1948 he was President of the Carnegie Endowment for International Peace, having been nominated to that position by the chairman of the board, John Foster Dulles. Americans were tremendously disturbed that such a man would be accused of serving as a Soviet Agent.

Throughout the hearings and trials which followed, Alger Hiss flatly denied the charges made against him by his former associate, Whittaker Chambers. Eventually, however, the famous "pumpkin papers" were turned over to the FBI and it was proven that the films of many highly secret documents had been copied on the Hiss typewriter in preparation for transmittal to Russia. Hiss was sentenced to five years for perjury. A comprehensive digest of the entire Hiss case may be found in *Seeds of Treason* by Ralph de Toledano (Chicago: Henry Regnery, 1962).

Whittaker Chambers eventually wrote a detailed analysis of how he was trapped by Communism and what it did to both himself and Hiss. His book is called *Witness* (New York: Random House, 1952).

THE KOREAN WAR, THE FIRING OF MacARTHUR AND THE JENNER COMMITTEE REPORT

Once Dr. Quigley had pointed out that the secret policy of the Establishment was to push the United States into a collectivist one-world society, it became increasingly, clear why so many White House and State Department decisions played directly into the hands of the Soviet strategists.

Consider, for example the pattern of the Korean War. Once China had fallen, the hopes of Korea, Formosa and Southeast Asia depended on the post-war committments of the U. S. to protect them. But in January, 1950, Dean Acheson announced that Korea, Formosa and the territory lying beyond were no longer within the "defense perimeter" of the United States. Within six months, Russia launched an attack against little South Korea, using the Communists of North Korea as a facade. (For an inside story on the way the Russians ran the entire Korean War, see "Russians in Korea: the Hidden Bosses," by Pawel Monat, *Life* Magazine, June, 1960, pp. 76-102).

In all U. S. history, Americans had never fought a war as frustrating as the war in Korea. After a brilliant initial victory under astonishing odds, General MacArthur defeated and captured the North Korean army. He then commenced the mopping up process in North Korea and suddenly found his forces unexpectedly confronted by several hundred thousand "volunteer" Red Chinese. For over four months MacArthur was not allowed to tell the American people that we were engaged in a whole new war and the enemy was now Red China. Chiang Kai-shek pleaded for an opportunity to liberate his country now that the Chinese were involved, but he had to depend on U. S. aid and was forbidden to move. General MacArthur was not even allowed to bomb the Yalu Bridge over which the Red Chinese were pouring their men and supplies. Nor was he allowed to attack the Chinese bases beyond the Yalu. After four months, a Congressman

OWEN LATTIMORE

wrote McArthur to find out why there were so many casualties when the war was supposed to be virtually over. The General frankly told the Congressman what had happened and when the Congressman read the letter on the floor of the House, it blew the political lid off of Washington. Within five days, General Douglas McArthur had been withdrawn from all commands in the Pacific.

The war lumbered along for two more years, but after Stalin died and an armistice was arranged, it was found that the U.S. Generals and Admirals had been deliberately prevented from winning the Korean War, even when there were several excellent opportunities to do so. Little did Americans know that we were supposed to have lost South Korea. Owen Lattimore, a principal strategist for the Institute of Pacific Relations in the betrayal of China, had written an article in the New York *Daily Compass,* July 17, 1949, stating that the idea was to let South Korea fall, but not let it look as though we pushed her.

On July 30, 1953, the famous Jenner Report came out of the Senate Judiciary Committee entitled: "Interlocking Subversion In Government Departments." This was right at the time the Establishment was trying to hush up or discredit the McCarthy hearings so the Jenner Report was given an extremely cool treatment by the liberal press. Here are the twelve conclusions of the Jenner Report which carried with them tragic implications in view of what has happened during all the years since:

"1. The Soviet international organization has carried on a successful and important penetration of the United States Government and this penetration has not been fully exposed.

"2. This penetration has extended from the lower ranks to top-level policy and operating positions in our Government.

78

"3. The agents of this penetration have operated in accordance with a distinct design fashioned by their Soviet superiors.

"4. Members of this conspiracy helped to get each other into Government, helped each other to rise in Government and protected each other from exposure.

"5. The general pattern of this penetration was first into agencies concerned with economic recovery, then to warmaking agencies, then to agencies concerned with foreign policy and postwar planning, but always moving to the focal point of national concern.

"6. In general, the Communists who infiltrated our Government worked behind the scenes—guiding research and preparing memoranda on which basic American policies were set, writing speeches for Cabinet officers, influencing congressional investigations, drafting laws, manipulating administrative reorganizations—always serving the interest of their Soviet superiors.

"7. Thousands of diplomatic, political, military, scientific, and economic secrets of the United States have been stolen by Soviet agents in our Government and other persons closely connected with the Communists.

"8. Despite the fact that the Federal Bureau of Investigation and other security agencies had reported extensive information about this Communist penetration, little was done by the executive branch to interrupt the Soviet operatives in their ascent in Government until congressional committees brought forth to public light the facts of the conspiracy.

"9. Powerful groups and individuals within the executive branch were at work obstructing and weakening the effort to eliminate Soviet agents from positions in Government.

"10. Members of this conspiracy repeatedly swore to oaths denying Communist Party membership when seeking appointments, transfers, and promotions and these falsifications have, in virtually every case, gone unpunished.

"11. The control that the American Communications Association, a Communist-directed union, maintains over communication lines vital to the national defense poses a threat to the security of this country.

"12. Policies and programs laid down by members of this Soviet conspiracy are still in effect within our Government and constitute a continuing hazard to our national security."

This reviewer talked with Senator Jenner on one occasion following these hearings. He said: "We were accused of seeing Communists under every bed, but that isn't true. What we saw were Communists IN the bed of nearly every Bureau in Washington."

Dr. Bella Dodd, former member of the National Committee of the Communist Party, told this reviewer that the Party estimated it had trained over 3,000,000 persons in Communist tactics and strategy by 1950, and that most of these had maintained a working relationship with the Party, or followed the Party line, even though many of them were no longer "dues-paying members."

THE McCARTHY HEARINGS

For several years the U. S. Congress tried to use its powers under the Constitution to compel the Executive Branch of the Government to clean out the subversives. Under the principle of checks-and-balances, the Congress can have its committees conduct investigations to determine whether or not there is corruption, waste of expenditures or subversion in the executive branch. Three avenues are open to the House and the Senate:

1. Upon learning of an allegation of subversion, refer it to the President or to the Department involved •and ask for an investigation and a report.

2. If this doesn't get results, then subpoena those who are supposed to know about the problem and release the facts to the public so there will be sufficient pressure and embarrassment to bring about a prompt improvement.

3. If neither of the above get results, then subpoena those who are known by other Government employees to be guilty of subversion and ask them under oath whether or not the charges are true. If such persons are innocent, they can say so; but if they plead the Fifth Amendment, then they will be publicly exposed and forced out of Government.

By 1950 the first two approaches had been used repeatedly with no results except contemptuous indifference. This reviewer has a published copy of a letter to the Secretary of State dated June 10, 1947, from the Senate Appropriations Committee, which states:

"It becomes necessary due to the gravity of the situation to call your attention to a condition that developed and still flourishes in the State Department under the administration of Dean Acheson.

"It is evident that there is a deliberate, calculated program being carried out not only to protect Communist personnel in high places, but to reduce security and intelligence protection to a nullity. . . .

"On file in the Department [of State] is a copy of a preliminary report of the FBI on Soviet espionage activities in the United States, which involves a large number of State Department employees, some in high official positions. This report has been challenged and ignored by those charged with the responsibility of administering the Department with the apparent tacit approval of Mr. Acheson. Should this case break before the State Department acts, it will be a national disgrace."

Nothing happened. Here was a committee in the Senate with a majority of its members being Democrats, pleading with its own Administration to clean house before there was a public scandal.

It can be readily understood

DEAN ACHESON

why more and more Congressmen and Senators decided by 1950 that it was high time they started naming names and calling persons accused of wartime subversion before an investigating Committee where they could either clear themselves or plead the Fifth Amendment, thereby indicating that they could not answer to the charges without incriminating themselves. This whole procedure was inaugurated by the Founding Fathers to get the facts without subjecting the accused to imprisonment in case he were guilty. In other words, the guilt of the person was revealed by his plea of the Fifth Amendment; but this could not be used against him in any criminal proceedings.

It was February 9, 1950, that a U. S. Senator decided to demand direct interrogation of alleged subversives. His name was Joseph McCarthy.

McCarthy was born on a farm near Appleton, Wisconsin, left school at age 14, entered high school at 20, graduated, enrolled in Marquette University and eventually graduated in law. Thereafter he was elected a circuit judge, but when World War II broke out he enlisted in the Marines and spent most of his military career in the South Pacific as an intelligence officer. He flew over 25 missions photographing targets from the back seat of dive-bombers or as a gunner on regular bomber planes. After the war he ran for the Senate against the most powerful politician in Wisconsin, Senator "Young Bob" Lafallette, who had been in the Senate for 21 years. McCarthy out-campaigned Lafallette and won by a substantial margin in one of the major political upsets of 1946. (For an intimate and sometimes critical biography of Joseph McCarthy, see *McCarthy* by Roy Cohn, The New American Library, New York, 1968.)

This reviewer has read many volumes on the McCarthy controversy and has discovered that you can learn very little from people like Dr. Quigley who, as we shall see in a moment, practically went into an intellectual spasm because McCarthy ALMOST aroused the American people to action against the Communist-Establishment conspiracy before they could get him politically quarantined. It turns out that McCarthy was neither the personification of Satan which the Establishment press (and Dr. Quigley) tried to picture him as being, nor was he the knight on a white charger which his defenders sometimes tried to present him as being. Actually, he was a tough, frustrated American ex-Marine who was sick and tired of seeing the enemy in striped pants walking around Washington sabotaging the most basic ingredients of America's interests both at home and abroad. It was in this spirit that he gave three speeches in 1950.

JOSEPH McCARTHY LAUNCHES A ONE-MAN CAMPAIGN

At Wheeling, West Virginia, Salt Lake City and Reno, Nevada, McCarthy talked about a letter which Secretary of State Byrnes wrote in 1946 to Congressman Adolph Sabath, stating that there were 284 people in the State Department who were "unfit." McCarthy had learned from confidential informants who had come to him from the State Department that as of 1950, 205 of these "unfit" persons were still there. He was told the names of 57 who were either Communists or loyal to the Communist Party and an additional group (making the total 81) who were marginal suspects.

The fact that McCarthy had the actual names of 57 identified subversives sent the State Department and the Establishment Press into a frenzy. McCarthy sent a wire to President Truman offering to furnish him the names of the 57, and suggested that the President require Dean Acheson to explain why these and the remainder of the 205 "unfit" persons were still in the State Department. The President never even acknowledged the wire.

The diversionary tactic used by the press and the defenders of the State Department was to accuse McCarthy of not being consistent with his figures. Was he charging the State Department with having 57 Communists, 81 Communists or 205 Communists? He was accused of being reckless and irresponsible in his charges.

McCarthy next went to the Senate and gave a speech offering to turn these 57 names—which he already had in his possession—over to a Senate Committee. McCarthy said he could furnish the names of witnesses who could positively

JOSEPH McCARTHY

identify these people as participating in subversive activities. The Senate appointed the Tydings Committee to hear McCarthy's charges. The Committee ended up investigating McCarthy. McCarthy went to the hearings prepared to present his "facts" and during the first day's session he was allowed barely 8 minutes of direct testimony. The next day he had 9½ minutes. Senator Tydings harangued the press and engaged in polemics which frustrated the entire proceedings. Tydings finally issued a "report" declaring McCarthy's charges a complete fake. McCarthy was beginning to learn what it meant to take on the Establishment. The storm signals were up and the liberal press, radio and TV immediately prepared to launch an all-out campaign to smash the senator from Wisconsin. Meanwhile, the 57 "identified" people inside the State Department were brought up before a Loyalty Board so the cases against them could be heard. 54 promptly resigned. By November 1954, not only had the original 57 been dismissed or resigned, but the same thing had happened to the 24 marginal cases which McCarthy had named in his figure of 81. (Dr. Quigley elected not to mention this in his book.)

IN 1953 McCARTHY BECOMES CHAIRMAN OF HIS OWN COMMITTEE

As a result of the Republican victory in 1952, Joseph McCarthy became chairman of the Senate's permanent Investigations Subcommittee. The Committee had a statutory mandate to investigate graft, incompetence and disloyalty cases. McCarthy took this assignment seriously. In 1953 he conducted 169 executive and public hearings and interrogated more than five hundred witnesses. Here is a summary of the findings:

1. That security laws and procedures in the State Department had become a farce.
2. That Establishment people at the White House and the top level of the State Department were continually employing people in spite of the fact that they came under the ban of "security risks."
3. That administrators and security officers who were demanding strict enforcement of security measures had been removed or transferred.
4. That "security risk" people who were either known Communists or Communist sympathizers were being made commissioned officers.
5. That people known to be Communist activists were advanced in the military even though the U.S. was fighting a Communist foe in Korea.
6. That the political pressures on the military resulted in people being commissioned and promoted even though these people had written "Fifth Amendment" on their loyalty oath form.
7. That an investigation of the Voice of America exposed waste, corruption and incompetence resulting in an immediate saving to the American people of some 18 million dollars.
8. That an investigation of the overseas libraries of the U. S. Information Service resulted in the removal of more than 30,000 Communist and Left-wing books.
9. That the hearings uncovered widespread Communist infiltration of the Government Printing Office and resulted

in the removal—or referral to the FBI—of more than 75 persons, and a complete reorganizing of the GPO security system.

10. That the investigation of Communist infiltration in key defense plants resulted in the suspension or discharge of more than 20 Fifth-Amendment security risk cases.

11. That the investigation exposed the existence of powerful Communist espionage cells operating in the secret radar laboratories of the Army Signal Corps at Fort Monmouth, N. J. (Although the FBI had been warning the Army about this situation since 1949, it was not until 1953 that McCarthy provided the ammunition which allowed a courageous commanding officer, Major General Kirke Lawton, to risk the wrath of top political brass by suspending 35 security risks. Amazingly, the Loyalty Review Board at the Pentagon reinstated all but two of these exposed security risks and gave them back-pay! McCarthy then demanded the names of the twenty civilians on this review board, and soon found himself sawing on a raw nerve of the most powerful Establishment team in Washington—the White House, the State Department, and the Pentagon.)

THE FAMOUS ZWICKER CASE

Nothing so outraged McCarthy in the Monmouth investigation as his discovery that an identified member of a Communist cell had been knowingly promoted from captain to major and had then been hurriedly given an honorable "separation" on orders of the White House after McCarthy had called the seriousness of this case to the attention of top military leaders. The man who had been promoted was Irving Peress of the dental corps at Camp Kilmer, N.J. The man who signed his "honorable separation" was General Ralph W. Zwicker.

It all began on January 30, 1954, when McCarthy called Major Peress to answer questions about his Communist affiliations. Peress invoked the Fifth Amendment 20 different times. It even turned out that Peress had written "Fifth Amendment" across his Loyalty Oath form and still had been promoted. It was unbelievable.

Finally McCarthy was ready for General Zwicker. This turned out to be a game of charades. The General was evasive and on occasion defiant. He changed his testimony three times under oath when asked if he knew who had ordered the general to give Peress his honorable separation.

But the general soon found, as other hostile witnesses had discovered in other hearings, that McCarthy was no "genteel Senatorial sophisticate." He was primarily an ex-Marine who had seen enough of subversion and corruption in certain military-White House-State Department policies to alert him to the fact that there are some very real enemies in the American camp. He didn't care whether they wore striped pants or army uniforms. If they were covering up for known Communists in the U.S. Military services, they were serving the enemy. When Zwicker turned hostile and treated the Committee with evasive contempt, McCarthy went after him like a prosecuting attorney. Strategically, it was a mistake. It gave McCarthy's enemies the ammunition they had been looking for. The payoff came after Zwicker refused to answer questions about Peress on the grounds that President Eisenhower had issued the same kind of restrictive order that President Truman had issued: no government employee could answer questions or supply Congressional committees with files relating to the loyalty of another government employee. Naturally, this short-circuited the whole checks-and-balance relationship between the legislative and executive branches of government, but there it stood.

McCarthy then asked General Zwicker if he thought a general who had knowingly covered up for a Communist should be removed from his command. General Zwicker said he didn't think that was sufficient reason to remove a general. Ex-Marine McCarthy was quick to react to that one. He immediately said: "Then, General, you should be removed from any command. Any man who has been given the honor of being promoted to general and who says 'I will protect another general who protected Communists' is not fit to wear that uniform, General."

That did it. McCarthy's enemies had their ammunition.

McCarthy was never allowed to continue his investigation. A whole series of charges were hurled against both McCarthy and the members of his staff. Time and energy were all absorbed in explaining or refuting a continuous avalanche of allegations. He was investigated five times in four years.

Finally the tidal wave of propaganda had reached a crescendo and the whole Establishment press as well as the Establishment hard-core in the Senate began to clamor for a censure. The Communist *Daily*

Worker published an instruction kit on how to get McCarthy. It was advertised as "Four full pages on Sen. Joe Low-Blow McCarthy, his record and what you can do about him."

Two graduate students from Yale decided to take a cold, hard look at the various McCarthy hearings and then examine the charges one by one. They found a variety of things for which they criticized Senator McCarthy but decided that without a doubt there was a con- certed campaign to deceive the American people as to the actual issues. They wrote a book entitled, *McCarthy And His Enemies* (Chicago: Henry Regnery Co., 1954). The authors were William F. Buckley and L. Brent Bozell. This book contains an excellent analysis of each of the charges against McCarthy. It even gives a case-by-case report on the people who were supposed to be smeared or improperly treated. Later an excellent analysis of the Zwicker case was written by Lionel Lokos entitled, *Who Promoted Peress?* (New York: The Bookmailer Press, 1961.)

THE CAMPAIGN TO CENSURE McCARTHY

It was not just the hearings of the McCarthy committee that got the Senator into trouble. He had also given a speech in which he documented what he called "Twenty Years of Treason" by Democratic administrations. Then he took on President Eisenhower's administration and charged it with continuing along similar if not identical lines. He had also put into the Congressional Record of June 14, 1951, a devas- tating attack on the State Department which was later published as *America's Retreat From Victory* (New York: Devin-Adair Co., 1951). The text relied upon published records to explain to the American people what the Communist-Establishment had done to the United States and her allies during the post-war years. It was a hard-hitting factual exposure of many top political, military and diplomatic personalities who had been surreptitiously carrying out the very policies which Dr. Carroll Quigley says the secret Establishment powers were using to gradually move humanity toward a global collectivist society.

And, of course, from the Establishment's point of view it was difficult if not impossible to refute McCarthy's charges against top Democrats and top Republicans who had been involved in these subversive activities. So they didn't try. Both groups simply combined in an all-out campaign to get McCarthy censured so that his charges could be DISCREDITED. That was the real tragedy of the McCarthy censure. It successfully distracted the American people from the real issues which could have turned the tide of history against the Communist-Establishment coalition.

Senator McCarthy was a bombastic type of personality and had his faults, but even his faults had to be inflated and exaggerated out of all reasonable dimensions before the heat of resentment could be generated to a level where the Senate would officially censure him. In fact, when the campaign against McCarthy first began, the Senator was confronted by the anomaly of seeing many of those who spoke out against him publicly, later apologizing to him privately and commending him for doing a good job. The Establishment press had created such a climate of "hate McCarthy" that even those who felt he was doing a good job found it politically expedient to denounce him.

When the Senate censure committee was appointed, it contained some questionable ingredients. One member had publicly stated even before he had heard the facts that he would vote to censure McCarthy. McCarthy attempted to object to that Senator's participation on the Committee, but was gavelled down by the Chairman. The Liberal press practically fell all over itself trying to applaud the chairman for having the manifest courage to "stand up" to McCarthy. Because the chairman was a friend of this reviewer, it was greatly disturbing to see him being "set up and trapped", in a historical sense, by the same people who were trying to discredit McCarthy.

Altogether, 46 charges were brought against McCarthy. They all dissolved into thin air except two. It was found that Senator McCarthy had "failed to cooperate" with a Senate subcommittee on Privileges and Elections in 1952 and that McCarthy had "intemperately abused" General Ralph W. Zwicker.

On the first count McCarthy offered an explanation which was not accepted, but which a subsequent investigation verified as being true. His attorney, Edward Bennett Williams, wrote a book in 1962 called *One Man's Freedom* in which he demonstrated that if McCarthy had been able to dig up certain information in time, the first count would have died along with the other 44 "dismissed" charges.

As for McCarthy's "intemperate" statement to General Zwicker, this was indeed a flimsy excuse for a censure. As researchers have since demonstrated, Senators of both the past and present have been using far more vigorous language against hostile witnesses without anyone raising the slightest objection.

And what about the censure of General Zwicker? What about the promotion of a known Communist and his being given a hasty honorable separation? What about giving commissions to security risks who wrote "Fifth Amendment" on their Loyalty Oath forms? What about the toleration of spy cells in highly secret military operations for several years after the FBI had warned of their existence?

Soon after these events General Zwicker was enjoying a pleasant retirement. It was only Senator Joseph McCarthy who got the censure. And it did accomplish *exactly* what the Communist-Establishment coalition intended.

From then until now, the people of the United States have been paying in blood and treasure for the historical mistake of letting the "censure of McCarthy" totally discredit the shocking disclosures which the McCarthy hearings had proven. Ever since then any one attempting to tell the truth about Communist subversion in America has run the risk of being accused of the most heinous of offenses—"McCarthyism!"

DR. CARROLL QUIGLEY ON McCARTHY

The reader of *Tragedy And Hope* will never learn that anything good came from the McCarthy hearings. He will never know it was one of those rare moments of awakening when the American people ALMOST became exposed to enough white light of reality to change the calamitous course of current history. It was such a narrow squeak for the secret power-combine that Dr. Quigley could not resist the urge to lash out at McCarthy with the most vehement kind of denunciation. Imagine this professional historian supposedly disciplined in the reporting of facts indulging in the following diatribe against "Satan" McCarthy:

"McCarthy was not a conservative, still less a reactionary. He was a fragment of elemental force, a throwback to primeval chaos. He was the enemy of all order and of all authority, with no respect, or even understanding, for principles, laws, regulations, or rules. As such, he had nothing to do with rationality or generality. Concepts, logic, distinctions of categories were completely outside his world. It is, for example, perfectly clear that he did not have any idea of what a Communist was, still less of Communism itself, and he did not care. This was simply a term he used in his game of personal power. Most of the terms which have been applied to him such as 'truculent,'

89

'brutal,' 'ignorant,' 'sadistic,' 'foul-mouthed,' 'brash,' are quite correct but not quite in the sense that his enemies applied them, because they assumed that these qualities and distinctions had meaning in his world as they did in their own. They did not, because his behavior was all an act, the things he did to gain the experience he wanted, that is, the feeling of power, of creating fear, of destroying the rules, and of winning attention and admiration for doing so. . . .

"His thirst for power was insatiable because, like hunger, it was a daily need. It had nothing to do with the power of authority or regulated discipline, but the personal power of a sadist. All his destructive instincts were against anything established, the wealthy, the educated, the well mannered, the rules of the Senate, the American party system, the rules of fair play. As such, he had no conception of truth or the distinction between it and falsehood, just as he had no conception of yesterday, today, tomorrow as distinct entities. . . ." (pp. 928-929)

This goes on for several more pages. It literally drips with malevolence. Dr. Quigley attempts to give a few "facts" from McCarthy's biography. Everything is solid black.

Cooler heads without any axe to grind have described McCarthy as aggressive and sometimes bombastic, but not a "throwback to primeval chaos." Like all politicians they have caught him in an occasional exaggeration, but his speeches and Committee reports certainly do not support the charge that his mind had "nothing to do with rationality or had no conception of truth or the distinction between truth and falsehood." In fact, the record would rather show that it was his ability to hammer home a whole panorama of irrefutable facts and present them in a completely rational, understandable way, that made him such an enemy of the powers behind the scenes. McCarthy was one politician who could make himself easily understood. And the American people were beginning to respond. That is what was so reprehensible to the Establishment.

The charge that he sought publicity begs the point. Every Congressional committee which feels it has an important message to get to the rest of Congress and the people will seek publicity. The point is whether or not the publicity was warranted. And was it accurate? From the point of view of any old-fashioned Constitution-oriented American, the McCarthy hearings were not only important, they were enough to leave the reader in a state of shock. As for their accuracy, what else can you deduct from a high government official who is asked whether or not he is part of the Communist conspiracy, and he pleads the Fifth Amendment? Why is it inaccurate to say that such a man has the earmarks of a "security risk?"

Quigley points out that in five years McCarthy did not prove that any person in the State Department was a Communist (p. 932). If he means in court, this is true. But *that* is the job of the Department of Justice, not a Congressional committee. The McCarthy hearings exposed enemies of the American people in high places. McCarthy's committee then recommended that more rigorous security laws be adopted. That was all his Senatorial Committee was supposed to do.

Dr. Quigley's statement that McCarthy "did not know what a Communist was," is completely irresponsible. Note that Quigley documents practically nothing throughout his entire book. What CAN be documented is the fact that McCarthy was finding not only Communists, but those who were hiring Communists, promoting Communists, hiding Communists and lying under oath to protect Communists.

After the McCarthy episode the American people virtually went back to sleep. Nevertheless, the spectre of Communism returned to haunt them again and again.

In 1955 it was the Formosa crisis.

In 1956 it was the Suez Canal crisis followed shortly by the tragic and disgraceful handling of the Hungarian Revolution.

In 1957 the State Department sponsorship of Fidel Castro as the George Washington of Cuba set the stage for the betrayal of Cuba and her 6 million allies to a brutal Communist conquest.

In 1958 the Soviet Union sponsored Nasser in the conquest of two independent Arab states. U.S. Marines had to land in Lebanon and both the British and U.S. had to combine to prevent the conquest of Jordan.

In 1959, the fall of Cuba had become a bizarre reality. While Castro was brutally communizing this island 90 miles from U.S. soil, the State Department was continuing to trumpet the deliberate falsehood that Castro was not really a Communist. The man on the Cuban desk of the State Department was himself a personal friend of Fidel Castro and a former member of the ABC Revolutionary Movement of Cuba.

PRELUDE TO A SHOWDOWN

It was Cuba as much as any other single factor which made the blood of Americans boil and caused the people of the United States to turn away from the Republicans in the election of 1960.

About the same time a few Americans among both Republicans and Democrats had begun to do their homework on the Communist conspiracy. A solid front of pro-American anti-Communists had begun to emerge from among America's long-suffering silent majority.

In 1958, J. Edgar Hoover came out with his *Masters of Deceit* and during the same year this reviewer's book was published under the title of *The Naked Communist.* By 1961 both books were on the national best-seller list.

Study groups, seminars, radio and TV broadcasts began springing up all over the country. Soon names such as Dr. George S. Benson, Dean Manion, Dan Smoot, Dr. Fred Schwarz, Robert Welch, and Billy James Hargis had become familiar to readers and reviewers in the mass communications media. It was a grass roots movement which, unknown to its participants, was racing toward a head-on collision with the Communist-Establishment coalition.

This reviewer was invited to serve on several of the faculties which were organized to speak at high schools, colleges and community gatherings. Everywhere the crowds were tremendous. Herbert Philbrick and the writer were teamed together to speak to audiences which sometimes totalled more than 10,000 in a single day. The week-long seminars had the same success.

Beginning in Los Angeles with an average attendance of only 200, the seminars increased until a year later we were meeting in the Los Angeles Sports Arena with daily attendance running into several thousand. Our speakers were presented on television each evening with sponsors paying for two and three hours of expensive TV time.

On October 16, 1961, the biggest anti-Communist rally in the history of the country was held in the Hollywood Bowl with a filmed telecast which subsequently went from coast-to-coast. The rally lasted three hours and was called "Hollywood's Answer to Communism." The stage was filled with the executives of the major studios and many of the top stars. George Murphy (later U.S. Senator) was the master of ceremonies.

This rally practically monopolized the TV audience in every area where it was shown. In many cities it was rebroadcast. New York saw it twice.

The rally had four speakers. They were Senator Thomas Dodd, Congressman Walter Judd, Dr. Fred Schwarz and the writer. Before we went on, one of the top executives of *Life* magazine asked for a few moments time.

Life had been ridiculing these seminars in recent editorials, but when advertisers began canceling contracts running into hundreds of thousands of dollars, C. D. Jackson rushed out to Hollywood to appear on the program and assure the country that *Life* also wanted to be counted among the patriots.

When my turn came to speak something unexpected occurred. It was my assignment to outline some of the practical steps which could be taken to protect the American people from further Communist subversion. My first suggestion was that we demand a full-scale, bipartisan investigation of the entire U.S. State Department. The crowd rose up in such a roar of approval that they virtually took over the program. Several minutes passed before they sat down again. Four other suggestions were also greeted with overtures of approval, but it was clearly evident that the investigation of the State Department was number one on their list. As we learned later, it was this particular part of the broadcast which upset the Establishment more than anything else.

Within just a few days there was a tremendous reaction from New York.

THE REUTHER MEMORANDUM

In retrospect it would seem that we had caught the Establishment somewhat by surprise. But not for long. Walter Reuther and his brother, Victor, who used to write back from Russia during their training days: "Carry on the fight for a Soviet America!" saw the telecast of the Hollywood Bowl rally when it was shown in New York. Being two of the Establishment's most powerful labor leaders (and principal behind-the-scenes strategists), they quickly drew up a plan of action. They wrote an extensive memorandum to the Attorney General, Robert Kennedy, outlining the steps which should be taken to promptly stop this highly embarrassing exposure of the inner sanctum. Not since the days of Senator Joseph McCarthy had the members of the secret power-combine been so emotionally disturbed.

Of course, to members of the Establishment, their global socialist society represents the ultimate dream in human achievement. Therefore, to them, we anti-Communist Americans look like reactionary conspirators who are guilty of postponing the communal millennium

WALTER REUTHER

with our old-fashioned Constitutional concepts of freedom and self-determination.

Fortunately, the Attorney General's office was kind enough to furnish a friend of the writer a copy of the Reuther Memorandum. Since then, it has been published. It speaks rather bitterly of the Hollywood rally:

"In Schwarz's Southern California meetings, as shown in the New York re-telecast a couple of weeks ago, Senator Dodd's and Representative Judd's heavy handed foreign policy polemics received little applause, but when W. Cleon Skousen (author of 'The Naked Communist') charged treason in high places, the place went up in a roar of applause." (Reuther Memorandum, p. 8)

This is not quite accurate, but the Reuther brothers were trying to make a point. Actually both Senator Dodd and Congressman Judd received excellent applause for their talks. What bothered the Reuthers was the fact that when I suggested investigating the State Department, the audience rose to its feet and vigorously demonstrated before the millions of TV viewers their hearty approval. The Reuthers could see a tide of American indignation rising at the grass-roots level. Since this is the key to exposing and deflating the power of the Establishment, it was imperative that we be taken off the air. A few speeches to local audiences wouldn't hurt much, but a television exposure to millions could soon make the Establishment so contemptible that every Congressman and Senator who was found supporting it would be replaced at the next election.

And that is exactly what we had in mind.

But for the moment, they drove us back to the grass-roots. The Reuther brothers recommended five tactical maneuvers which turned out to be temporarily devastating to the grass-roots movement:

1. Muzzle the military by having all speeches cleared through a military and State Department censuring committee.

2. Use every means possible to stop the flow of funds to

94

conservative organizations. Use Internal Revenue to investigate conservative organizations and remove their tax-exemption where possible.

3. Use the power of the Federal Communications Commission to regulate (eliminate) conservative programs.

4. Have conservative organizations placed on the Attorney General's "Subversive Organizations" list in order to provide a "balanced list."

5. Curb the activities of J. Edgar Hoover who "exaggerates the domestic Communist menace . . . and contributes to the public's frame of mind."

VICTOR REUTHER

WASHINGTON'S CAMPAIGN TO STOMP OUT CONSERVATIVE EDUCATIONAL PROGRAMS

The muzzling of the military came almost immediately. Furthermore, all patriotic and anti-Communist military programs were suspended. Leading military officials who resisted or objected were forced into retirement or given disciplinary assignments. The Reuthers made their position clear in their memorandum:

"The radical right inside the Armed Services presents an immediate and special problem requiring immediate and special measures. . . .

". . . the spectacle of the U. S. Army sponsoring Skousen's reflection on the patriotism of Franklin Roosevelt and the loyalty of Harry Hopkins, could only have been achieved through the connivance of inside military personnel." (Reuther Memorandum, pp. 10-11)

It was clear that as of 1961 the Establishment didn't want people to know about Harry Hopkins giving atomic secrets to the Soviets any more than it had in the days of Joseph McCarthy.

Using the Internal Revenue to harrass patriotic organizations and their leaders was also promptly implemented. By using technical decisions (and sometimes reversing previous decisions) the IRS was able to assess Walter Knott of Knotts Berry Farm a fortune in taxes.

Billy James Hargis was told that his organization was having its tax-exempt status suspended because of participation in politics. Of course, no such ruling would ever be applied to the Ford Foundation's Fund for the Republic.

This reviewer was small fry but likewise received a visit from IRS. I gained the impression, however, that the examiner knew he was on a vindictive "political" assignment. In any event, he seemed rather pleased when he returned some time later to announce that after going over my records, he had discovered that the Government owed me several hundred dollars!

As far as getting the patriotic educational programs off the air, that was amazingly successful. They did it through the FCC "Fairness Doctrine." This provided that if you paid for a program and mentioned subversive individuals or organizations who had been exposed by Congressional committees, those individuals or organizations could demand equal time FREE OF CHARGE to answer. Theoretically the idea sounded perfectly "fair," but in practice it resulted in all stations excluding any programs which made SPECIFIC references to people or organizations which had been involved in subversive activities. All future programs had to be in terms of generalities. Education in broad principles continued on the air, but actual exposure of the subversion being uncovered by Congressional Committees practically died. Station managers were afraid they would go broke giving free time to those who wanted to answer. Had the "Fairness Doctrine" required the stations to offer paid time to the offended party, there would have been no problem. But, of course, that would not have fulfilled the objective of the Reuther Memorandum.

THE KENNEDY YEARS

There had been several things in the John F. Kennedy campaign which had led some people to expect his administration to be an improvement over the last years of Eisenhower. At least, he had promised to "do something about Cuba." But, as Dr. Quigley boasts, "Kennedy despite his Irish Catholicism, was an Establishment figure." (p. 1245) Instead of conditions improving the calamities began to escalate. Here are some examples:

As early as 1960, the U.S. Communist leader, Gus Hall, had announced that the Party was going to alienate and radicalize the American Youth. Within a short time, Castro beards, hippy clothes, filthy speech, Communist salutes, Communist songs, Communist peace symbols, drugs, pornography, nihilism and riots became the order of the day.

In 1961 the American image dropped at least a thousand points with the Bay of Pigs debacle. When this writer lectured in South America, there was a constant demand for an explanation of the immoral decision to allow 1,400 Cuban freedom-fighters to walk into what could have been a virtual massacre without telling them of the decision by President Kennedy to withdraw the promised U.S. air cover.

Afterwards, the world watched in amazement as the mighty United States allowed itself to be blackmailed into raising a ransom of millions of dollars worth of drugs and other goods in order to get the Bay of Pigs survivors back to the United States.

1962 brought the Cuban missile crisis, because the Kennedy administration allowed the Soviet Union to mount their ICBM's behind our defense lines and within target range of the entire United States. The warning speeches of Senator Keating of New York were almost contemptuously ignored until the President went on an election campaign tour and found his own party members booing when he mentioned Cuba. He cancelled the rest of his trip, raced back to Washington and immediately announced that a missile site had been photographed by a U-2 plane. This writer was serving on the Free Cuba Committee and knew that a map of known missile silos had been drawn up by Cubans working on the Soviet project and that this map had been furnished to the President and the Pentagon over a year earlier. The map even showed the number and location of Soviet troops, but knowledge of any such Soviet forces continued to be publicly denied in Washington.

When the existence of the missiles was finally established there was a demonstration of profound concern. The President announced to Khruschev that the missiles and military personnel must be removed immediately and that the United States would conduct an on-the-spot examination to make certain the stipulation was carried out. It was the kind of a speech Americans had been anxious to hear. But after the election was over, the most pathetic display of accommodation was

97

ROBERT KENNEDY AND JOHN KENNEDY

exhibited by Washington as the Soviets went through the motions of
pretending that the missiles had been removed. Not at any time was
there any inspection, and the same Cuban informants who told Senator
Keating about the missiles in the first place continued to insist that
many of them were still there.

In 1963 the Left-wing forces induced President Kennedy to
recommend the passage of a whole series of hard-core socialist proposals
and these were soon dumped into the hoppers of Congress. However,
there were sufficient Americans awake at the grass-roots level to protest
against these measures and demand that Congress reject them. That is
what happened. Even under Presidential pressure the Democratic-
dominated Congress refused to pass these bills. The frustrated Establishment press turned the heat on Congress but to no avail. By September
the prestige of President Kennedy had taken a serious drop in
Establishment circles and there was some question as to what might
happen if JFK decided to seek a second term. Then suddenly, on
November 22, President Kennedy was assassinated by a Marxist
revolutionary, Lee Harvey Oswald, who was connected with Castro's

main Communist front-organization here in the United States.

Under the emotional shock of this tragic event, the Establishment realized the nation might react politically and demand that the whole Soviet-Communist apparatus be outlawed. Establishment spokesmen such as Earl Warren immediately blamed the President's murder on the "Radical Right," but when the arrest of Oswald revealed that it had been done by the Radical Left, the Left-wing machinery went into high gear to assure the American people that Oswald could not, by any stretch of the imagination, be part of an international Communist plot. He must be accepted as merely an isolated psychopathic individual who acted on his own initiative. To prevent any independent investigation by anti-Communist Democrats and Republicans, the Communist *Daily Worker* suggested that President Johnson appoint a special commission to do the investigating with Earl Warren as chairman. Four days later that was precisely what President Johnson did. The real story of the Kennedy assassination was soon buried beneath an Establishment-supervised white-wash designed to pacify the American people.

When Congress convened in 1964, President Johnson obliged the Left-wing elements of his party by exploiting the emotional climate resulting from the President's death and demanded that the Congress pass the Kennedy bills which they had rejected the previous spring. Almost blindly the Congress went to work and frequently, without any serious attempt to debate many important aspects of these bills, they began to be passed.

At the grass-roots, observing citizens of both political parties became increasingly alarmed with what they could see happening. They began scouring the political field for a candidate who could rally the American people and re-direct the course of the nation before it was too late.

Foremost among the conservative candidates, of course, was Barry Goldwater, the Senator from Arizona. For several years he had been saying that America was off the track and had to go back. History was catching up with the American people and what he had been saying began to make more and more sense. This was bound to reflect itself politically so it was not long before the Goldwater-for-President campaign started to roll. All across the country delegates to the Republican National Convention began announcing in advance that they had made an iron-clad commitment to support Goldwater and ONLY Goldwater.

THE 1964 REPUBLICAN CONVENTION AND THE GOLDWATER CAMPAIGN

SENATOR BARRY GOLDWATER

The political climate of 1964 was such that a capable conservative candidate had an excellent chance of winning, and the Establishment knew it. Money and manpower was thrown into the primaries and individual state organizations to try to stop Goldwater before he ever got to San Francisco but the Goldwater bandwagon continued rolling along. The next step was to try to stop him at San Francisco.

The Establishment forces at the Republican National Convention were represented by the Rockefeller-Scranton contingents. They used every political weapon in their well-furbished arsenal to embarrass or discredit Goldwater. To veteran political observers it was amazing how strong the locked-in Goldwater delegates stood up under the pressure. Goldwater was nominated.

The Establishment then turned to its own locked-in sources of power. The media (press, radio and TV) were turned on Goldwater with a blazing vengeance. In retrospect it was an amazing demonstration of what a controlled press can do in a free republic. The tactic was to divert the attention of the people away from the real issues and use whatever circumstances became available to FRIGHTEN the American people away from Goldwater.

In Stephen Shadegg's book, *What Happened to Goldwater?* (New York: Holt Rinehart and Winston, 1965) there is a valuable summary of the factors which determined the ultimate outcome of the Goldwater campaign. Shedegg points out that it was impossible for Goldwater to be heard on the issues when the press, the magazines, the radio and TV were all pounding out a subtle (and sometimes blatant) message of "Extremist," "Racist," "Atomic-bomber," "Trigger Happy," "Warmonger," "Psychologically unfit," and "He will scrap social security."

Television advertising against Goldwater was also shrewdly prepared along the same theme. It included two powerful little Madison Avenue gems, one showing an atomic explosion and the other showing a social security card being torn in two.

Shadegg writes: "A part of the answer to the question "What happened to Goldwater?" must be found in the violence of those who opposed him. The election did not hinge on the popularity or ability of Lyndon Johnson. He was a secondary figure, and the 'great mandate' became his inheritance. It was not a testament to his wisdom or leadership, but rather an indication of the violent dislike for Goldwater generated largely by the hundreds of magazine articles, the

LYNDON B. JOHNSON

derogatory remarks of the columnists, the unexplained errors (such as the UPI report of Goldwater's statement on the Howard Smith ABC television appearance), and the scathing attacks of people such as William Stringfellow, Ralph Ginsberg, and Fred Cook."

Dean Burch said:

"I think that most of the reporters, if they would ever let their defenses down, would agree that taken as a whole the press was so violently antagonistic to Goldwater that even if they had wanted to be honest about it, it was impossible for them to be honest because they were so busy looking for weaknesses. In other words, the press in this particular campaign performed the function of the opposition. They took a look at what Goldwater advocated and then they looked for whatever was the weakest link in that chain and that became the issue.

"On the other hand, with Johnson, anything that was against him they ignored. For example, if Senator Goldwater during his twelve years in the U.S. Senate had accumulated $14 million as a personal fortune, I am sure that the press in a period of three months could have made his name synonymous with Benedict Arnold, whereas with Johnson it was just one of those 'Well boys will be boys things and everyone is entitled to make a living.'

"Secondly, if I or someone close to Senator Goldwater had been called before the Senate Rules Committee and then taken the Fifth Amendment, that subject would never have been dropped. At every press conference Goldwater would have been asked to explain in detail what my role was, what he planned to do about it, whereas the Bobby Baker case was stressed ONLY BY GOLDWATER. THE PRESS NEVER DISCUSSED IT WITH THE PRESIDENT.

"Thirdly, if I had been picked up in the men's room of the YMCA, [like LBJ's man, Jenkins] the stories that would have been written on it would have lasted for two or three months and the conclusion would have been that obviously Goldwater knew about it and obviously, possibly, he was a little bit peculiar." (*What Happened To Goldwater*, pp. 263-264)

In assessing the Goldwater campaign, some criticism must rest on certain members of the Goldwater team. Unfortunately for the conservative cause he represented, Goldwater operated under the special handicap of having two or three men immediately around him who were extremely inept. If Stephen Shadegg, who had run all of Goldwater's successful campaigns from 1952 to 1962, had been in charge, and Ronald Reagan had been presenting the Goldwater issues at regular intervals on coast-to-coast TV (as John Kilroy and his committee had the money and begged for permission to do), the propaganda of the Establishment-controlled media MIGHT have been overcome. As it was, a citizen had to be a strong independent thinker to survive the barrage of frightening headlines and slogans which the secret society and its power complex poured out against Goldwater.

Nevertheless, some 27,000,000 stood up against the barrage.

HUNTLEY-BRINKLEY ADMIT GOLDWATER COULD HAVE WON

A few months after the election, Huntley-Brinkley came out with an astonishing report. They said that if the election had been run strictly on the issues, Goldwater could have won! The program was narrated by Brinkley and he referred to a political survey in which it had been discovered that a good majority of the people agreed with

102

Goldwater in principle, but had been "influenced" into voting against him because of specific fears that he would do away with social security or get us involved in an atomic war. (In other words, the FRIGHT propaganda had robbed the people of their legitimate choice.)

As this reviewer watched this Huntley-Brinkley Special Report, it was difficult to understand why these dedicated employees of the power-complex media would admit how popular Goldwater had been and how he would have won the election if their propaganda efforts had not been so effective. However, Brinkley explained toward the end of the program why it was important for the "liberal, progressive" element of the country to appreciate that even though they had won the election, they had not changed the "conservative mood" at the grass roots. He said President Johnson would therefore have an uphill pull to get many of his "progressive" bills passed through Congress (just as the Democratic Congress had initially bucked President Kennedy's socialist legislation) unless all the liberal-progressive element firmly united to overcome the conservative, grass-roots resistance. This "Report" was obviously designed to keep the liberal minority from letting down as they usually do after a strenuous presidential campaign. It was essential that the Johnson administration be harnessed to the task which the central power-complex had in mind for it.

Ironically, however, the new President was harnessed to a team which intended to exploit him to the hilt and then abandon him before the next election. For three solid years the powers behind the scenes pushed the President into policies and programs which were bound to be resisted and resented by the majority of the American people and were therefore political dynamite. The most serious time-bomb which they planted on LBJ was getting him to follow a commitment of peace-at-any-price and a soft-on-Communism policy. This allowed the global planners to escalate the Vietnam front into a full-scale war and have the President fight it on such an unrealistic, no-win basis that it became the primary factor in making Lyndon Johnson a one-term president.

Added to this was the devastating political erosion of the TFX scandal, the problem of run-away inflation, the unprecedented sky-rocketing in crime, the irrational policy of trying to get integration by a series of provocative confrontations between blacks and whites, the resulting riots, burning, looting and killing, the indifference of the administration and its Supreme Court toward the tidal backwash of pornography, filthy speech and flagrant obscenities, and last—but by no means least—the credibility gap which left both the press and the public wondering when the administration was telling the truth and when it was telling calculated falsehoods.

As the time drew near for the 1968 election it became painfully clear what the master-planners had in mind for their erst-while leader, LBJ. Suddenly, and without the slightest hint as to their motivation, the Left-wing swung their polemic clubs at President Johnson. He was politically ripped to shreds by the very people who had originally pushed him into power. They had used him to gain all the mileage possible from his good offices and then once he had destroyed himself politically (by doing exactly what they had told him to do), they prepared to toss him aside for a far more radical candidate.

But the tragic ramifications of the Johnson story must wait to be told in detail on some other occasion. We must now get back to Dr. Quigley and see what he had to say about the Johnson-Goldwater election campaign.

DR. QUIGLEY'S AMAZING REACTION TO THE GOLDWATER PHENOMENON

It will be recalled how hysterically Dr. Carroll Quigley reacted to the McCarthy situation. Goldwater did the same thing to him. The possibility of the American people turning their backs on the trend toward socialism and actually longing again for the open fields and blue sky of a free society, practically sent Dr. Quigley into a psychological frenzy. It is rather astonishing to see him approach this type of problem as though he had received no training whatever as an objective historian. Suddenly he shuts his eyes and goes into imaginary flights of fanciful day-dreaming. Note how he feels compelled to explain Goldwater support only in terms of ignorance, stupidity and perfidy.

Dr. Quigley's Opinion Of Those Seeking to Preserve Traditional Americanism:

"His [Goldwater's] most ardent supporters were of the extremist *petty bourgeois* mentality DRIVEN TO NEAR HYSTERIA by the disintegration of the middle classes and the steady rise in prominence of EVERYTHING THEY CONSIDERED ANATHEMA: Catholics, Negroes, immigrants, intellectuals, aristocrats (and near aristocrats), scientists, and educated men generally, people from big cities or from the East, cosmopolitans and internationalists and, above all, liberals who accept diversity as a virtue." (p. 1248, emphasis added)

Transliterated, Quigley is saying that the most ardent supporters of Barry Goldwater were fanatical, small-time businessmen or clerical mentalities who had reached a state of hysteria over the fact that "their" middle class society was "collapsing." The glaring fact was that America's middle class had not been collapsing but was its fastest growing segment! Nevertheless, in the best tradition of Marx and Lenin, Quigley insists that the small property owner is a roadblock to progress and must be eventually eliminated (pp. 1234 to 1278). So Goldwater's supporters were from the collapsing middle class who hated Catholics (this writer has a lot of Catholic friends who aren't going to like being called anti-Catholic just because they voted for Goldwater!); against the Negroes (racists, you see); against the foreign born (actually these often make better conservatives and are more appreciative of America than some of the mixed-up heirs of wealthy U.S. bankers and industrialists); against the well-educated people from the big cities (because only ignorant country bumpkins could vote for a man like Goldwater, no doubt); against internationalists (on this point he is correct if he means international socialism and international Communism); and above all against those "liberals who accept diversity as a virtue." It is not "diversity" to which Goldwater supporters objected but the Left-wing insistence that we allow room for downright "subversion and treason" within our ranks.

So Goldwater's supporters were PETTY BOURGEOISIE. (Note these key words in the first sentence of the above quotation.) It makes one think he might be reading Karl Marx or V. I. Lenin again. To make certain nobody misses the point, Dr. Quigley shares with us his personal definition of this non-American term which comes straight out of Marxist propaganda.

Dr. Quigley Defines Petty Bourgeoisie:

"The second most numerous group in the United States is the petty bourgeoisie, including millions of persons who regard themselves as middle class and are under all the middle class anxieties and pressures, but often earn less money than unionized laborers. As a result of these things, they are often VERY INSECURE, ENVIOUS, FILLED WITH HATREDS, AND ARE GENERALLY THE CHIEF RECRUITS FOR ANY RADICAL RIGHT, FASCIST, OR HATE CAMPAIGNS against any group that is different or which refuses to conform to middle-class values. Made up of clerks, shopkeepers, and vast numbers of office workers in business, government, finance, and education, these tend to regard their whitecollar status as the chief value in life, and live in an atmosphere of envy, pettiness, insecurity, and frustration. They form the major portion of the Republican Party's supporters in the towns of America, as they did for the Nazis in Germany thirty years ago." (pp. 1243-44)

A lot of people will now know exactly what Dr. Quigley thinks of THEM! Insipient Nazis, no less.

Of course, he does admit that there were some rather substantial people (financially speaking) who supported Goldwater, but he assures us that they were primarily the "new rich" who were "unbelievably ignorant and misinformed." (p. 1247) In fact, Dr. Quigley has some interesting things to say about the contest between the "new rich" and the "old wealth" who represent the Establishment. Note how Dr. Quigley finds it impossible to discuss any opposition to his favorite global collectivist friends without putting it on a basis of angels vs. the devils.

Quigley's Theory That the Goldwater Campaign Was a Struggle Between the "Old Rich" and the "New Rich":

"At issue here was the whole future face of America, for the older wealth stood for values and aims close to the Western traditions of diversity, tolerance, human rights and values, freedom, and the rest of it, while the newer wealth stood for the narrow and fear-racked aims of petty-bourgeois insecurity and egocentricity." (p. 1246)

Dr. Quigley assures us that such a ragtag assortment of country bumpkins, petty bourgeoisie and ignorant "new rich" could never win over the city slickers of the Global Establishment. He equates this low-bred contingent of Americans as the "neo-isolationists" who constitute a threat to the modern world. They are modern man's cultural enemy and therefore his political enemy. In other words, the global collectivists offer modern man his only hope. Anyone who stands in the way is an evil omen of tragedy. Dr. Quigley is certain, however, that the Global Establishment has the brains and the resources to put down any Americans like McCarthy or Goldwater who have the audacity to suggest that America restore the basic Constitutional concepts on which she was built and eliminate from public life those who have been subverting them. Dr. Quigley says it is a contest between the amateurs and the professionals. Note the air of disdain and smug superiority in the following quotation concerning the success of the Establishment in suppressing opposition during the early 1950's.

Quigley Feels Middle Class "Neo-Isolationist" Americans Can Always Be Beaten By Establishment Forces:

"On the whole, the neo-isolationist discontent [another of Dr. Quigley's epithets for ordinary Americans who object to what the Establishment has been doing to them] was a revolt of the ignorant against the informed or educated, of the nineteenth century against the insoluble problems of the twentieth, of the Midwest of Tom Sawyer against the cosmopolitan East of J. P. Morgan and Company, of old Siwash against Harvard, of the *Chicago Tribune* against the *Washington Post* or *The New York Times,* of simple absolutes against complex relativisms, of immediate final solutions against long-range partial alleviations, of frontier activism against European thought, a rejection out of hand, of all the complexities of life which had arisen since 1915 in favor of a nostalgic return to the simplicities of 1905, and above all a desire to get back to the inexpensive, thoughtless, and irresponsible international security of 1880." (pp. 979-980)

In this quotation Dr. Quigley clearly sets the stage for the coming conflict between traditional Americans and the powerful secret combination of the Global Establishment. Dr. Quigley has no doubt in his mind as to the final outcome. He equates hope and progress with the Establishment, tragedy and horse-and-buggy backwardness with traditional Americanism.

Of course, if you go to Washington, New York, the United Nations Headquarters, or to the capitals of any major nation in the world you will find massive evidence that Dr. Quigley has a basis for his bias. His people are everywhere. And they ARE running things.

Let's take a look at one or two of these groups in action.

THE BILDERBERG GROUP—AN EXAMPLE OF DR. QUIGLEY'S GLOBAL ESTABLISHMENT IN ACTION

Every once in awhile, the network lets down its guard long enough for us to get a slight but alarming peek into the inward parts of the mammoth machine which Dr. Quigley believes is now too big to stop. When one contemplates the interlocking global ramifications which this power structure had developed, it is little wonder that Dr. Quigley feels so tremendously confident about its ultimate and irrevocable victory. Nevertheless, we shall have something to say about this in a moment.

Meanwhile, let us take a look at some of the "conferences"

called by the global establishment. These are held each year as an international master planning conclave. They are secret and attendance is restricted to invited "guests." These turn out to be about 100 men from the top inner circle representing their four major dimensions of power: the international banking dynasties, their corporations involved in vast, international enterprises, the American tax-exempt foundations, and the establishment representatives who have gained high offices in government, especially the United States government.

These conferences always have the same chairman—his royal highness Prince Bernhard of the Netherlands, who, with his family, owns a massive fortune in the Royal Dutch Shell Oil Corporation. Then, close at hand, will always be David Rockefeller representing his family and especially Standard Oil of New Jersey which is one of the largest corporate structures in existence. It is interesting that in the past two decades when political revolutions have occurred in various parts of the world, these two companies usually end up with all of the oil and natural gas concessions. This has been largely true in Africa, the Middle East, South America and the Far East. These are also the companies whose installations seem to be virtually off limits to the bombers in both sides of any recent war. We mention this simply to demonstrate the fact that Dr. Quigley does seem to be correct in alleging that the political and economic forces of the earth are being woven into a gigantic monolith of total global power. As Raymond B. Fosdick, one of those who nearly always attends these Bilderberg conferences, has said, the Bilderberg partners are spinning "the infinity of threads (economically and politically) which bind peace together." (Quoted in *The Review of the News,* September 21, 1966, p. 22) And of course the "peace" they have in mind is compulsive cooperation, which a socialized world government could enforce upon humanity to the exclusion of any significant resistance—hence there would be peace as THEY envision it.

Prince Bernhard convened the first of these conferences during May, 1954, at the Bilderberg Hotel in Oosterbeek, Netherlands, Ever since then the group has been called The Bilderberg Group. However, they meet at various places. The 1957 meeting was held off the coast of Georgia on St. Simons Island, not far from Jekyl Island where a secret meeting was held in 1908 to set up the format for the U.S. Federal Reserve Bank. The 1964 meetings were at Williamsburg, Va. They have also met in Canada, Turkey, Germany, England and France. All of their meetings are closed. No secretary takes notes of the speeches. No reporters sit in on the debates. And when Prince Bernhard brings down the gavel for the close of the conference, no handouts, policy statements or copies of their adopted resolutions are given to the press. The conferees depart to the four corners of the earth to carry out their adopted goals but the world is never given the slightest hint as to what has been decided. This is particularly frustrating to Congress which has tried several times to ferret out the activities of these Bilderberg conferences. Even when top government officials such as Navy Secretary, Paul Nitze, were placed under oath and interrogated, it became virtually impossible to learn anything of significance.

PRINCE BERNHARD

The only press representatives in attendance have been trusted Establishment personalities such as Arthur Hays Sulzberger, president and publisher of the *New York Times,* Ralph E. McGill, pro-Castro editor of the *Atlanta Constitution,* Gardner Cowles, editor and publisher of *Look* magazine, and C. D. Jackson, of *Life* magazine (the same C. D. Jackson who appeared on "Hollywood's Answer to Communism" in 1961 and tried to placate advertisers who had cancelled hundreds of thousands of dollars in advertising when *Life* editorially attacked the anti-Communist movement).

Apparently, the great fear of the Bilderberg Group has been the possibility of infiltration and exposure. They therefore sometimes make a pretense of publicizing their meetings and even acknowledging who has been invited so that the presence of so many world-renowned personalities will not look quite so conspiratorial or mysterious. At least this has helped to demonstrate who is represented at these conferences and what political and economic allies are banding together.

Here, for example, in addition to these already mentioned, are typical individuals who frequent these conferences:

Joseph E. Johnson, President of the Carnegie Endowment for International Peace (which finances most of these conferences).

Dr. Joseph H. Retinger, Communist Poland's Charge d'Affaires in Russia who helped Prince Bernhard set up the first conference in 1954.

McGeorge Bundy, former Harvard professor who became a presidential advisor and was then made President of the Ford Foundation.

George W. Ball, former Under Secretary of State.

109

Christian Herter, former Secretary of State

Dean Acheson, former Secretary of State.

Dean Rusk, former Secretary of State and former President of the Rockefeller Foundation.

Lester Pearson, former Prime Minister of Canada.

Shepard Stone, Director of International Affairs for the Ford Foundation.

Pierre-Paul Schweitzer, Managing Director of the United Nations International Monetary Fund.

Dirk U. Stikker, Secretary General of NATO.

Gardner Cowles, editor in chief and publisher of *Look* magazine and the Cowles Newspaper chain.

J. William Fulbright, U.S. Senator of Arkansas and author of the famous Fulbright Memorandum which resulted in the muzzling of the military so they could not discuss the Communist threat and who called on the United States to "accept Red Cuba."

Paul G. Hoffman, U.S. chief of foreign aid who later became the architect for the dispersion of the Ford Foundation funds and then went on to head the United Nations Special Fund.

George F. Kennan, former ambassador to the Soviet Union.

Paul H. Nitze, who served as Secretary of the Navy.

Fritz Berg, Chairman, Federation of German Industries.

Hakon Christianson, Chairman of the Board, East Asiatic Company of Denmark.

Pierre Commin, Secretary of the French Socialist Party.

Thomas E. Dewey, former Governor of New York and candidate for President.

Jacob Javits, Republican Senator from New York.

H. J. Heinz II, President of the H. J. Heinz Company.

Jeane de la Garde, French Ambassador to Mexico.

M. Nuri Birgi, Minister of Foreign Affairs, Turkey.

Imbriani Longo, Director-General, Banco Nazionale del Lavoro, of Italy.

David J. McDonald, President United Steelworkers.

Alex W. Menne, President Association of German Chemical industries.

Don K. Price, Russian Institute, Columbia University.

J. L. S. Steele, Chairman, British International Chamber of Commerce.

Paul van Zeeland, former Prime Minister of Belgium.

John J. McCloy, former President of the Chase-Manhattan Bank.

Henry Kissinger, advisor to President Nixon, former member of the staff of CRF and an officer of the Rockefeller Fund.

Perhaps this is enough to represent the width and breadth of global influence which is present when the Bilderberg Group is called into session.

THE PUGWASH CONFERENCES

The student of Dr. Quigley's global establishment should also be familiar with another facet of the power struggle—the Pugwash Conferences. These are the pride and joy of the Canadian-American multimillionaire, Cyrus Eaton.

Cyrus Eaton was born in Nova Scotia but became a naturalized U. S. citizen. He began his career

HENRY A. KISSINGER

with John D. Rockefeller, Sr., and eventually became a successful financial tycoon in public utilities, steel, banking, railroading, mining, and the paint industry. Eaton's interests have included the Republic Steel Corporation, Otis & Company, the Sherwin-Williams Company, and Baltimore and Ohio Railway, the Chesapeake and Ohio Railway, and various utility companies in both Canada and the United States. His son's company, Tower International, Inc., has joined with the Rockefeller brothers' International Basic Economy Corporation, to promote trade between the Communist bloc and the United States, Canada and Latin America.

Cyrus Eaton is committed to the proposition that the Soviet Union and the United States must be amalgamated. He is host to prominent Communist officials whenever they visit the United States and he is a frequent visitor to the iron curtain countries.

In 1954 Eaton dedicated his ancestral home at Pugwash, Nova Scotia, as a retreat for intellectuals of his liking. In 1957, he helped

CYRUS EATON

develop the first formal Pugwash Conference attended by more than twenty of the world's best-known nuclear scientists. They came from the United States, Canada, Australia, France, Japan, Britain, Austria, Communist Poland, Communist China, and the Soviet Union. What exchange of top-secret nuclear information took place will never be known unless one of these participants someday decides to disclose it.

Since 1957, more than a dozen Pugwash conferences have been held in various parts of the world, including Communist countries. All of them have been attended by high officials of the last four administrations. Much of the discussion has centered around ways and means of getting the United States to disarm.

Cyrus Eaton has labored tirelessly for U.S. diplomatic recognition of Red China and is the recipient of the Lenin Peace Prize—an award reserved exclusively for those who have made highly significant contributions to the advancement of the interests of the Soviet Union.

Obviously, the Bilderbergers, Pugwash conferees, and other master-planners of the global establishment have a lot of things going for them.

SO WHERE DOES ALL OF THIS LEAVE TRADITIONAL AMERICANS?

As I see it, the great contribution which Dr. Carroll Quigley unintentionally made by writing *Tragedy And Hope* was to help the ordinary American realize the utter contempt which the network leaders have for ordinary people. Human beings are treated *en masse* as helpless puppets on an international chess board where giants of economic and political power subject them to wars, revolution, civil strife, confiscation, subversion, indoctrination, manipulation and outright deception as it suits their fancy and their concocted schemes for world domination.

But, as we have previously mentioned, this MASS of world humanity is precisely the source of latent power which terrifies the Establishment. There is the constant fear that the masses might awaken and frustrate their gigantic schemes, particularly where they have acquired an education and accumulated a little property (which gives them a highly significant degree of independence). That is what has happened to the mass of humanity in America. They now constitute the great and overwhelming majority of the people, called the middle class. And Dr. Quigley, as we have already seen, leaves no doubt as to the menace which middle-class Americans are believed to represent insofar as the Establishment is concerned.

It was once the great American dream to make as many people as possible a part of the great middle class because it was recognized to be the backbone of our society and the most important segment of the population in maintaining a progressive, self-governing, secure, and freedom-loving people. But, obviously, if you are trying to set up a virtual dictatorship, this group is an enemy. This group will resist a dictatorship. At least, it will do so if it knows what is happening.

So this is the fact of life which the super-rich collectivists of the Establishment face today. Everything they do must be accomplished in an atmosphere of propaganda and deception. Otherwise they keep running into a groundswell of resentment and resistance as they try to compel middle class Americans to give up their independence, their property, and their constitutional prerogatives.

Then what is the current strategy of the Establishment? It is two-pronged.

PRESSURE FROM THE TOP AND PRESSURE FROM THE BOTTOM

The current tactic is to create revolution, violence and extremely serious social dislocation at the bottom while creating an ever-increasing pressure at the top for monolithic power by demanding that the executive branch of the Federal government be given massive power to "solve" all these problems. These demands are made in the form of proposed "social legislation" involving the expenditure of billions upon billions each year. Experience is teaching us, of course, that the dissipation of all this wealth has NOT been solving our problems. It has merely permitted the Establishment to use these tremendous resources to build up its machine of well-paid Establishment lackeys

113

and reward their abject obedience with fabulous salaries for loyally carrying out the policies and dictates of the Global Establishment on practically every dimension of the Federal government.

Naturally, many fine, well-meaning people support the broad ramifications of social legislation because they think they are supporting "a good cause." On first view and at close range, they seem to be right, but as time has gone by year after year it has gradually become alarmingly apparent what all this social legislation is doing to us.

Americans are losing control of their destiny.

Furthermore, many of the people whom we have been calling our national problem-solvers have been secretly engaged in actual problem making.

As this reviewer has watched the deterioration of the American political structure during the past several decades, it has been absolutely amazing to see how many of our so-called "problems" have been literally manufactured or seriously aggravated by Washington meddling and manipulating.

For example, we had the problem of racial minorities and the need to expose these minorities to greater opportunities to share in the good things of life. That problem needed to be solved. But what happened? Washington meddling practically promoted it into the explosive tinder for another civil war.

We had the problem of rising crime rates. These needed to be stopped. Establishment mentalities flooded the country with elaborate social schemes and grossly permissive judicial decisions which multiplied the crime rate and set the stage for the greatest wave of violence and lawlessness this country has ever known.

We had the problem of providing an adequate educational opportunity for all our children. Washington came up with a conglomorate of money and policies which have seriously discredited the public schools in many parts of the country and caused private schools to spring up like mushrooms.

We had the problem of moral decay and something needed to be done about it. The Establishment brain-busters came up with a combination of sex education and so-called sensitivity training which is exploding the problem into a contagion of totally permissive decadence and moral degeneracy.

We had the problem of pornography and obscenity. Washington smashed what little legal protection existed, and the country was immediately inundated with running tides of obscene filth and shot-gun blasts of four-letter gutter words peppering every dimension of our press and mass communications media.

We had a problem of subversion by a foreign-based conspiracy which had brazenly announced that our American society must be overthrown and our children be required to live under its flag. Grass-roots political pressure compelled the Congress to pass a number of security laws. Establishment-dominated forces in the executive and judicial branches of the government have now totally nullified them.

Surely our descendants who will reap a terrible whirlwind from all of this will wonder why the adults of this generation were incapable of realizing what was happening.

Actually, what we are witnessing is a very carefully and methodically executed program designed to destroy constitutional government as we have known it and make a shambles of the society which has wanted to keep the Constitution alive. Only then can a highly centralized, socialist state be established.

To achieve this, the middle class in America must be ruthlessly squeezed out of existence. That is the message which looms large from many passages in Dr. Quigley's book and which will be found as a favorite theme in the books, magazines and newspapers of the Establishment's liberal press. Just as Marx and Engels waged war against the middle class to set up a socialist state, so does Dr. Quigley and the global network.

The middle class is to be identified as the "petty bourgeoisie," the "neo-isolationists," the broad masses of Americans who are described by Dr. Quigley as "often very insecure, envious, filled with hatreds, and are generally the chief recruits for any Radical Right, fascists, or hate campaigns against any group that is different or which refuse to conform to middle-class values" (p. 1243). What are Middle-class values?

Middle-class values, of course, are represented by the Constitutional concepts of limited government, states rights, rights of property, a competitive economy, the solving of problems on the local level if possible and, in any event, with a minimal of government meddling. But all this, Dr. Quigley would seem to suggest, is anathema. It has to go. People who think this way are middle-class mentalities. They are described by Dr. Quigley as the same kind of people as those who supported "the Nazis in Germany thirty years ago" (p. 1244). Dr. Quigley offers no proof whatever for this fantastic contention but then one should not expect too much. THERE IS NOT A SINGLE

115

FOOTNOTE OF AUTHORITATIVE REFERENCE IN ALL 1,300 PAGES OF DR. QUIGLEY'S BOOK!

However, in passing, one might ask Dr. Quigley this question: "If the middle class in America is to disappear, where will all these masses go?"

The Establishment has provided the answer in its millions of pages of socialist-oriented literature. The doomed members of the middle class are promised that they will become the carefully nurtured, carefully housed, carefully educated, totally dependent class of Government wards in a man-made paradise of a one-world socialist state.

But what if it didn't work out, or what if they didn't like it? What if it turned out to be like Russia, or China, or Cuba? What if they didn't want to be totally dependent citizens in a one-world, socialist state?

Well, of course, all such thoughts are treasonous. They partake of the traditional American middle-class mentality. Such doubts are a form of paranoia and mental illness. All such people should be put away safely so as not to contaminate the rest of the great society. (No doubt you have read Orwell's *1984* or Dr. Brock Chisholm's recommendations for World Mental Health!)

But then there is always the haunting possibility that the great middle class in America might gradually awaken and decide to take remedial action before it is too late.

Or is it too late already? Dr. Quigley seems to think so.

As he disdainfully indicates in his book on page 979, the grass-roots resistance movement, even as far back as the Korean crisis, was never a match for the big boys who are really running things. He said it was like "the Midwest of Tom Sawyer against the cosmopolitan East of J. P. Morgan and Company, of old Siwash against Harvard, of the *Chicago Tribune* against the *Washington Post* or the *New York Times*. . . ." Dr. Quigley never leaves any doubt as to where the real power centers of the Global Establishment actually lie.

And, as seen through the eyes of Dr. Quigley, the sheer size and power of the world-wide, super-rich network is now too big and too well entrenched to be overturned, or even resisted effectively. Its members will go right ahead financing revolution, moral depravity and social dislocation at the bottom and then sanctimoniously and energetically promise to solve all these problems if we will just delegate to them total power at the top. This is the formula which the master-planners believe is unbeatable.

But this reviewer believes they could be wrong. Without discounting for a moment the terrifying proportions of the enemy's posture of power, they still could be beaten.

WHAT CAN BE DONE ABOUT IT?

Although millions of unsuspecting Americans have become be-numbed and bewitched by Global Establishment brain-washing, this reviewer feels there is still sufficient vitality among the people to mobilize a formidable wave of hard-core resistance to the whole super-structure of world-wide conspiracy.

One thing which we urgently needed was a book by some insider like Dr. Quigley which could assure the people that the international conspiracy for global control is as terribly real and as tragically close to achieving its purposes as it actually is. If this reviewer had written such a book it would have no doubt been brushed aside as merely the work of another middle-class American striking out feebly against the imponderable powers that be. But not so with Dr. Carroll Quigley. As a sympathetic insider, he has told it as it is. And for that we warmly thank him!

Now the task is to do something about it.

Possibly the next ten years will be the crucial period during which free men in general, and Americans in particular, will decide whether we have the stamina and intelligence to turn the tide. After that, it COULD be too late.

The future task is political in nature. Essentially, it is a matter of methodically and deliberately uniting the vast resources of political power at the grass roots level and "throwing the rascals out." Every Democrat, Republican or Independent from the top of the Federal government right down to the lowest official on the local level, who has been consistently supporting the collectivist policies and tactics of the global network, should be summarily replaced as fast as the electoral process will permit.

Public officials can no longer be equated in terms of "being nice," having a "wonderful TV personality," or merely making promises. Each one must be coldly examined in terms of his record. If he turns out to be a lackey of the Establishment, a fellow-traveler of the Establishment, or even a dupe, he has to go.

Establishment henchmen should all be replaced by men and women who are totally committed to restoring the American society to its

117

traditional position provided within the framework of the American Constitution as visualized by the founding fathers. If you study it carefully, you will find that practically every major problem facing the United States today is related in some fundamental way to a violation (or series of violations) of Constitutional principles. We had a great system going which somebody has betrayed.

Not only must the political puppets of the international network be replaced, but once the political climate has been improved we have a tremendous amount of restructuring to do.

For example, the conspiratorial enemy's power base must be eliminated. If anything can be drawn from a study of Dr. Quigley's *Tragedy And Hope,* it is the alarming fact that the whole monolithic, interlocking power structure of international finance is in flagrant violation of the general welfare of the people of the United States (not to mention the rest of the world!). This mammoth concentration of economic power is in direct opposition to the traditional American precept that, unless it has been specifically stated otherwise, all power of every sort must remain DISPERSED among the people. Therefore, laws must be passed so that the nightmarish monstrosity of credit and money power which has been rapidly gravitating into a few conspiring hands, can be decisively dismantled. This would also require that the Federal Reserve System (which is neither "Federal" nor a "Reserve") be eliminated and replaced with a fiscal structure which does not violate the fixed responsibilities of Government as set forth in Article I, Section 8, of the United States Constitution.

Eliminating the enemy's financial power base would immediately facilitate the recovery of lost ground in many other areas. It would allow us to liberate our captive press, radio and TV facilities so the people could be told what is really going on. It would facilitate the liberation of the captive public school system which, for many years, has been harnessed so effectively to the collectivist propaganda machinery. It would also facilitate the liberation of certain religious bodies, universities, and other powerful, opinion-molding channels which have been bought-over and corrupted by the fabulous wealth of the network's billion-dollar, tax-exempt foundations.

A fresh political climate would also permit us to rectify a serious political blunder which our nation committed back in 1945. At the close of World War II, the people of the United States felt there should be some type of alliance among peace-loving nations to help prevent future predatory wars. What the Establishment set up for us was a conglomorate of international intrigue designed to become the political, financial and military power base for the Establishment's passionate dream of a monolithic global government.

As a federation of peace-loving nations, the United Nations proved to be a hypocritical farce with the world's foremost proponent of war, subversion and world conquest written in as a charter member. The promise of the United Nations to protect small nations produced equally bitter fruit, and the United States found itself having to provide multi-billion-dollar-protection for the free world against Communist aggression so as to make up for the veto-ridden frustrations of the quarreling UN Security Council.

Most Americans have probably forgotten that it was the Soviet Union which insisted that the headquarters for the United Nations be set up in the United States, but of course, as Dr. Quigley points out, that was exactly the way Rhodes and Stead originally planned it (p. 133). It was also no small coincidence that the entire site for the United Nations headquarters was donated by the Rockefellers.

No doubt the American people would have been happy to see some kind of international arena provided where various disputes could be publicly ventilated. In fact, that is what they thought they were getting. However, the United Nations charter was written by a State Department-Soviet Union coalition of strategists who specifically designed the UN so that it could eventually override the sovereign independence of its member nations and subject them to the Marxist-dominated World Court and the Marxist-directed military forces of the United Nations.

Amazingly, Establishment-sponsored U. S. presidents from both the Democratic and Republican parties have endorsed this scheme to subjugate the United States (including its internal affairs) to the jurisdication of the World Court. Establishment spokesmen such as Senator J. William Fulbright (Rhodes Scholar) has advocated scrapping the Constitution, while presidential advisor, Walt W. Rostow (Rhodes Scholar), has proclaimed that the United States must prepare to give up its national sovereignty.

The hour is late. At this stage of America's historical development, no honest student of current events should have any difficulty recognizing that we have been involved in a deadly flirtation with national disaster.

Of course, if we are to build a genuine bulwark of political strength against the international network, it is essential that one of the national political parties be renovated and restructured as a base of operations for all Democrats and Republicans who sincerely want to preserve the Constitutional structure of the American nation. This can be done only by launching a nationwide educational program designed to eliminate much of the confusion which presently exists concerning each of the major parties.

For example, the Democratic Party has become popularly identified as the "people's" party, the "prosperity" party, the party of the poor, the down-trodden, the working man, and the distressed. In reality, it has been the party through which the Wall Street globalists and the Left-wing international conspiracy have accomplished most of their subversion of both the Constitution and the traditional pattern of life on which the American culture was founded.

Actually, the Democratic Party was originally the conservative party. It promised to guard the constitutional prerogatives of the people against the usurpation of power by big government. It stood for public frugality, a balanced budget, states rights, resistance to Wall Street monopolies and all the rest. In fact, this was the theme of the 1932 platform on which FDR was elected and this reviewer endorsed that platform and became a registered Democrat. But by 1936, a complete metamorphosis was taking place. Alfred E. Smith, standard-bearer of the Democrats in the 1928 presidential elections, announced in 1936 that the party had been deliberately betrayed into the hands of those who represented the Socialist-Left-wing camp. It has remained there ever since—promising, promising, taxing, taxing, spending, spending, electing, electing. Harry Hopkins said this was the magic formula by which the Democrats could continue in power indefinitely. In fact, Norman Thomas, the perennial Socialist Candidate for President, announced that there wasn't any need for a Socialist Party any more because the Democrats were doing practically everything the Socialists had been advocating. (See Appendix, Alfred E. Smith's "Betrayal of the Democratic Party.")

The Republicans, on the other hand, have been identified as the genuinely "conservative" party which it has NOT been for a full generation. Whenever it has been in power it has tried to out-do the Democrats in both spending and big government. Its leaders have been largely Establishment figures serving as a backstop for the Democrats in case the Democrats fell out of favor with the public. Establishment Republicans have always insisted that the ideological base of the party be stretched out far enough to include a powerful Left-wing segment because they claimed that was the only way to obtain or retain power.

Actually, the Republicans and conservative Democrats might take a hard look at the possibility of remaking the Republican Party into a genuine, American Constitutionalist Party and openly challenging the whole fabric of Left-wing betrayal regardless of whether it has been coming from Democrats or Republicans. At least, by restructuring the Republican Party it could be a place where men and women of honest convictions could rally without being betrayed by the Establishment's pseudo-Republicans.

Some have felt the necessity of pushing for a third, independent party and eventually this may be the only recourse. At the moment, however, and due to the shortness of time, it would appear to be more practical to restructure the traditional "conservative" party as a genuine hard-hitting defender of American institutions and American values and come out in the open for international cooperation while vigorously opposing international consolidation. It could be the party for responsible fiscal policies, the protection of property rights, the elimination of confiscatory taxation, the disengagement from international intrigue. It could be the means of restoring the people's confidence in the processes of representative government by providing more men and women of genuine integrity in the courts and other stations of public service.

To bring about these needed changes it is necessary to push to the surface a whole new breed of articulate, well-informed, tough-minded political leaders who have done their homework and are capable of taking on this gigantic international network of global power. Already a few such men and women are beginning to appear on the political scene. Some have already been elected to political office. This must become the wave of the future.

The job devolving on the rest of us is to encourage these courageous Americans who are willing to give up the peace and quiet of their personal lives in order to take on the stormy career of public service. We should encourage them with money, moral support, by doing our own homework, and by speaking up decisively to sustain the right when critical issues are being decided.

The job ahead is gigantic, but this reviewer believes that America's misused, much abused, silent majority can still turn back the prevailing tide of impending disaster.

It is time we got on with the task.

APPENDIX

BETRAYAL OF THE DEMOCRATIC PARTY

By

Alfred E. (Al) Smith

(Alfred E. Smith, Democratic governor of New York during four terms, became the Democratic candidate for President in 1928 but lost to Herbert Hoover. In 1932 he supported Franklin D. Roosevelt for President, but by 1936 he was so shocked and alarmed by what he saw happening that he decided to warn his Party. Because of the popularity of President Roosevelt this step was considered by some to be virtual treason. Nevertheless, on January 25, 1936, Alfred E. Smith gave the following speech in Washington, D.C., to warn the American people that the Democratic Party was being betrayed.)

At the outset of my remarks let me make one thing perfectly clear. I am not a candidate for any nomination by any party at any time, and what is more I do not intend to even lift my right hand to secure any nomination from any party at any time.

Further than that I have no axe to grind. There is nothing personal in this whole performance so far as I am concerned. I have no feeling against any man, woman or child in the United States. . . .

I was born in the Democratic party and I expect to die in it. And I was attracted to it in my youth because I was led to believe that no man owned it. Further than that, that no group of men owned it, but on the other hand, that it belonged to all the plain people in the United States.

PATRIOTISM ABOVE PARTISANSHIP

It is not easy for me to stand up here tonight and talk to the American people against the Democratic Administration. This is not easy. It hurts me. But I can call upon innumerable witnesses to testify to the fact that during my whole public life I put patriotism above partisanship. And when I see danger, I say danger, that is the "Stop, look, and listen" to the fundamental principles upon which this Government of ours was organized, it is difficult for me to refrain from speaking up.

What are these dangers that I see? The first is the arraignment of class against class. It has been freely predicted that if we were ever to have civil strife again in this country, it would come from the appeal to passion and prejudices that comes from the demagogues that would incite one class of our people against the other.

In my time I have met some good and bad industrialists. I have met some good and bad financiers, but I have also met some good and bad laborers, and this I know, that permanent prosperity is dependent upon both capital and labor alike.

And I also know that there can be no permanent prosperity in this country until industry is able to employ labor, and there certainly can be no permanent recovery upon any governmental theory of "soak the rich" or "soak the poor." . . .

122

A GOVERNMENT BY BUREAUCRATS

The next thing that I view as being dangerous to our national well-being is government by bureaucracy instead of what we have been taught to look for, government by law.

Just let me quote something from the President's message to Congress:

"In 34 months we have built up new instruments of public power in the hands of the people's government. This power is wholesome and proper, but in the hands of political puppets of an economic autocracy, such power would provide shackles for the liberties of our people."

Now I interpret that to mean, if you are going to have an autocrat, take me; but be very careful about the other fellow.

There is a complete answer to that, and it rises in the minds of the great rank and file, and that answer is just this: We will never in this country tolerate any laws that provide shackles for our people.

We don't want any autocrats, either in or out of office. We wouldn't even take a good one.

The next danger that is apparent to me is the vast building up of new bureaus of government, draining resources of our people in a common pool of redistributing them, not by any process of law, but by the whim of a bureaucratic autocracy.

THE 1932 PLATFORM

Well now, what am I here for? I am here not to find fault. Anybody can do that. I am here to make suggestions. What would I have my party do? I would have them reestablish and redeclare the principles that they put forth in that 1932 platform. . . .

The Republican platform was ten times as long. It was stuffy, it was unreadable, and in many points, not understandable. No Administration in the history of the country came into power with a more simple, a more clear, or a more inescapable mandate than did the party that was inaugurated on the Fourth of March in 1933.

And listen, no candidate in the history of the country ever pledged himself more unequivocally to his party platform than did the President who was inaugurated on that day.

Well, here we are!

Millions and millions of Democrats just like myself, all over the country, still believe in that platform. And what we want to know is why it wasn't carried out. . . .

Now, let us wander for awhile and let's take a look at that platform, and let's see what happened to it. Here is how it started out:

"We believe that a party platform is a covenant with the people, to be faithfully kept by the party when entrusted with power, and that the people are entitled to know in plain words the terms of contract to which they are asked to subscribe.

"The Democratic Party solemnly promises by appropriate action to put into effect the principles, policies and reforms herein advocated and to eradicate the political methods and practices herein condemned."

My friends, these are what we call fighting words. At the time that that platform went through the air and over the wire, the people of the United States were in the lowest possible depths of despair, and the Democratic platform looked to them like the star of hope; it looked like the rising sun in the East to the mariner on the bridge of a ship after a terrible night.

But what happened to it?

APPENDIX

ECONOMY IN GOVERNMENT

First plank: "We advocate immediate and drastic reduction of governmental expenditures by abolishing useless commissions and offices, consolidating departments and bureaus, and eliminating extravagance to accomplish a saving of not less than 25 per cent in the cost of the Federal Government."

Well, now, what is the fact? No offices were consolidated, no bureaus were eliminated, but on the other hand, the alphabet was exhausted. The creation of new departments—and this is sad news for the taxpayer—the cost, the ordinary cost, what we refer to as housekeeping cost, over and above all emergencies—that ordinary housekeeping cost of government is greater today than it has ever been in any time in the history of the republic.

THE UNBALANCED BUDGET

Another plank: "We favor maintenance of the national credit by a Federal budget annually balanced on the basis of accurate Federal estimate within revenue."

How can you balance a budget if you insist upon spending more money than you take in? Even the increased revenue won't go to balance the budget, because it is hocked before you receive it. What is worse than that? . . .

THE MIDDLE CLASS WILL PAY THE DEBT

Now here is something that I want to say to the rank and file. There are three classes of people in this country; there are the poor and the rich, and in between the two is what has often been referred to as the great backbone of America, that is the plain fellow.

That is the fellow that makes from one hundred dollars a month up to the man that draws down five or six thousand dollars a year.

Now, there is a great big army. Forget the rich; they can't pay this debt. If you took everything they have away from them, they couldn't pay it; they ain't got enough. There is no use talking about the poor; they will never pay it, because they have nothing.

This debt is going to be paid by that great big middle class that we refer to as the backbone and the rank and file, and the sin of it is they ain't going to know that they are paying it. It is going to come to them in the form of indirect and hidden taxation. It will come to them in the cost of living, in the cost of clothing, in the cost of every activity that they enter into, and because it is not a direct tax, they won't think they're paying, but, take it from me, they are going to pay it!

WHAT ABOUT STATES' RIGHTS?

Another plank: "We advocate the extension of Federal credit to the States to provide unemployment relief where the diminishing resources of the State make it impossible for them to provide for their needs."

That was pretty plain. That was a recognition in the national convention of the rights of the States. But how is it interpreted? The Federal Government took over most of the relief problems, some of them useful and most of them useless. They started out to prime the pump for industry in order to absorb the ranks of the unemployed, and at the end of three years their employment affirmative policy is absolutely nothing better than the negative policy of the Administration that preceded it.

"We favor unemployment and old age insurance under State laws."

Now let me make myself perfectly clear so that no demagogue or no crack-pot in the next week or so will be able to say anything about my attitude on this kind of legislation. I am in favor of it. And I take my hat off to no man in the United States on the question of legislation beneficial to the poor, the weak, the sick, or the afflicted, or women and children.

Because why? I started out a quarter of a century ago when I had very few followers in my State, and during that period I advocated, fought for, introduced as a legislator and finally as Governor for eight long years, signed more progressive legislation in the interest of the men, women and children than any man in the State of New York

UNCONSTITUTIONAL MEASURE–UNFULFILLED PLEDGES

And the sin of this whole thing, and the part of it that worries me and gives me concern, is that this haphazard, hurry-up passage of legislation is never going to accomplish the purposes for which it was designed and–bear this in mind, follow the platform–under State laws. . . .

Another one: "We promise the removal of Government from all fields of private enterprise except where necessary to develop public works and national resources in the common interest."

NRA! A vast octopus set up by government, that wound its arms around all the business of the country, paralyzed big business, and choked little business to death.

Did you read in the papers a short time ago where somebody said that business was going to get a breathing spell?

What is the meaning of that? And where did that expression arise?

I'll tell you where it comes from. It comes from the prize ring. When the aggressor is punching the head off the other fellow he suddenly takes compassion on him and he gives him a breathing spell before he delivers the knockout wallop.

WASTEFUL EXTRAVAGANCE

Here is another one: "We condemn the open and covert resistance of administrative officials to every effort made by congressional committees to curtail the extravagant expenditures of Government and improvident subsidies granted to private interests."

Now, just between ourselves, do you know any administrative officer that has tried to stop Congress from appropriating money? Do you think there has been any desire on the part of Congress to curtail appropriations?

Why, not at all. The fact is that Congress threw them right and left—didn't even tell what they were for.

And the truth, further, is that every administrative officer sought to get all that he possibly could in order to expand the activities of his own office and throw the money of the people right and left. And as to subsidies, why, never at any time in the history of this or any other country were there so many subsidies granted to private groups, and on such a huge scale.

The fact of the matter is that most of the cases now pending before the United States Supreme Court revolve around the point whether or not it is proper for Congress to tax all the people to pay subsidies to a particular group.

Here is another one: "We condemn the extravagance of the Farm Board, its disastrous action which made the Government a speculator of farm products, and the unsound policy of restricting agricultural products to the demand of domestic markets." . . .

What about the restriction of our agricultural products and the demands of the market? Why, the fact about that is that we shut out entirely the farm market,

125

and by plowing under corn and wheat and the destruction of foodstuffs, food from foreign countries has been pouring into our American markets—food that should have been purchased by us from our own farmers.

In other words, while some of the countries of the Old World were attempting to drive the wolf of hunger from the doormat, the United States flew in the face of God's bounty and destroyed its own foodstuffs. There can be no question about that.

Now I could go on indefinitely with some of the other planks. They are unimportant, and the radio time will not permit it. But just let me sum up this way. Regulation of the Stock Exchange and the repeal of the Eighteenth Amendment, plus one or two **minor planks** of the platform that in no way touch the daily life of our people, have been carried out, but the balance of the platform was thrown in the wastebasket. About that there can be no question.

Let's see how it was carried out. Make a test for yourself. Just get the platform of the Democratic Party, and get the platform of the Socialist Party, and lay them down on your dining room table, side by side, and get a heavy lead pencil and scratch out the word "Democrat," and scratch out the word "Socialist," and let the two platforms lay there.

Then study the record of the present Administration up to date. After you have done that, make your mind up to pick up the platform that more nearly squares with the record, and you will put your hand on the Socialist platform. You don't dare touch the Democratic platform.

DEMOCRATIC OR SOCIALISTIC?

And incidentally, let me say, that it is not the first time in recorded history, that a group of men have stolen the livery of the church to do the work of the devil.

Now, after studying this whole situation, you will find that that is at the bottom of all our troubles. This country was organized on the principles of representative democracy, and you can't mix **Socialism or Communism** with that. They are like oil and water; they refuse to mix.

And incidentally, let me say to you, that is the reason why the United States Supreme Court is working overtime throwing the alphabet out of the window— three letters at a time.

Now I am going to let you in on something else. How do you suppose all this happened? Here is the way it happened. **The young Brain Trusters caught the Socialists in swimming and they ran away with their clothes.**

Now, it is all right with me. It is all right to me if they want to disguise themselves as Norman Thomas or Karl Marx, or Lenin, or any of the rest of that bunch, but what I won't stand for is to let them march under the banner of Jefferson, Jackson, or Cleveland.

"WE CAN TAKE A WALK"

Now what is worrying me, where does that leave me as a Democrat? My mind is now fixed upon the Convention in June, in Philadelphia. The committee on resolutions is about to report, and the preamble to the platform is:

"We, the representatives of the Democratic Party in Convention assembled, heartily endorse the Democratic Administration."

What happens to the disciples of Jefferson and Jackson and Cleveland when that resolution is read out? Why, for us it is a washout. There is only one of two things we can do. We can either take on the mantle of hypocrisy or we can take a walk, and we will probably do the latter.

Now leave the platform alone for a little while. What about this attack that has been made upon the fundamental institutions of this country? Who threatens them, and did we have any warning of this threat? Why, you don't have to study party platforms. You don't have to read books. You don't have to listen to professors of economics. You can find the whole thing incorporated in the greatest declaration of political principles that ever came from the hands of man, the Declaration of Independence and the Constitution of the United States.

CONSTITUTIONAL LIMITATIONS

Always have in your minds that the Constitution and the first ten amendments to it were drafted by refugees and by sons of refugees, by men with bitter memories of European oppression and hardship, by men who brought to this country and handed down to their descendants an abiding fear of the bitterness and all the hatred of the Old World was distilled in our Constitution into the purest democracy that the world has ever known.

There are just three principles, and in the interest of brevity, I will read them. I can read them quicker than talk them.

"First, a Federal Government, strictly limited in its power, with all other powers except those expressly mentioned reserved to the States and to the people, so as to insure State's rights, guarantee home rule, and preserve freedom of individual initiative and local control."

That is simple enough. The difference between the State constitutions and the Federal Constitution is that in the State you can do anything you want to do provided it is not prohibited by the Constitution. But in the Federal Government, according to that government, you can do only that which that Constitution tells you that you can do.

What is the trouble? Congress has overstepped its bounds. It went beyond that Constitutional limitation, and it has enacted laws that not only violate the home rule and the State's right principle—and who says that? Do I say it? Not at all. That was said by the United States Supreme Court in the last ten or twelve days.

CHORUS OF YES-MEN IN CONGRESS

Secondly, the Government, with three independent branches, Congress to make the laws, the Executive to execute them, the Supreme Court, and so forth. You know that.

In the name of Heaven, where is the independence of Congress? Why, they just laid right down. They are flatter on the Congressional floor than the rug on the table here. They surrendered all of their powers to the Executive, and that is the reason why you read in the newspapers references to Congress as the Rubber Stamp Congress.

We all know that the most important bills were drafted by the Brain Trusters, and sent over to Congress and passed by Congress without consideration, without debate and, without meaning any offense at all to my Democratic brethren in Congress, I think I can safely say without 90 per cent of them knowing what was in the bills.

That was the meaning of the list that came over, and besides certain bills were "Must." What does that mean? Speaking for the rank and file of American people we don't want any executive to tell Congress what it must do, and we don't want any Congress or the Executive jointly or severally to tell the United States Supreme Court what it must do!

And further than that, we don't want the United States Supreme Court to tell either of them what they must do.

127

APPENDIX

What we want, and what we insist upon, and what we are going to have is the absolute preservation of this balance of power which is the keystone, the arch upon which the whole theory of democratic government has got to rest. When you rattle that you rattle the whole structure.

Of course, when our forefathers wrote the Constitution of the United States it couldn't be possible that they had it in their minds that it was going to be all right for all time to come. So they said, "Now, we will provide a manner and method of amending it."

That is set forth in the document itself, and during our national life we amended it many times.

We amended it once by mistake, and we corrected it. What did we do? We took the amendment out. Fine, that is the way we want to do it, by recourse to the people.

But we don't want an Administration that takes a shot at it in the dark and that ducks away from it and dodges away from it and tries to put something over in contradiction of it upon any theory that there is going to be a great public howl in favor of that something; possibly the United States Supreme Court may be intimidated into a friendly opinion with respect to it.

What I have held all during my public life is that Almighty God is with this country, and He didn't give us that kind of Supreme Court.

Now this is pretty tough on me to have to go at my own party this way, but I submit that there is a limit to blind loyalty.

As a young man in the Democratic Party, I witnessed the rise and fall of Bryan and Bryanism, and I know exactly what Bryan did to our party. I knew how long it took to build it after he got finished with it. But let me say this to the everlasting credit of Bryan and the men that followed him, they had the nerve and the courage and honesty to put into the platform just what their leaders stood for. And they further put the American people into a position of making an intelligent choice when they went to the polls.

Why, the fact of this whole thing is—I speak now not only of the executive but of the legislature at the same time—that they promised one set of things; they repudiated that promise, and they launched off on a program of action totally different.

Well, in 25 years of experience I have known both parties to fail to carry out some of the planks in their platform. But this is the first time that I have known a party, upon such a huge scale, not only not to carry out the plank, but to do the directly opposite thing to what they promised.

SUGGESTED REMEDIES

Now, suggestions, and I make these as a Democrat anxious for the success of my party, and I make them in good faith.

No. 1: I suggest to the members of my party on Capitol Hill here in Washington that they take their minds off the Tuesday that follows the first Monday in November. Just take their minds off it to the end that you may do the right thing and not the expedient thing.

Next, I suggest to them that they dig up the 1932 platform from the grave that they buried it in, read it over, and study it, breathe life into it, and follow it in legislative and executive action, to the end that they make good their promises to the American people when they put forth that platform and the candidate that stood upon it 100 per cent. In short, make good!

Next, I suggest to them that they stop compromising with the fundamental principles laid down by Jackson and Jefferson and Cleveland.

AL SMITH AND FRANKLIN D. ROOSEVELT – 1932

Fourth: Stop attempting to alter the form and structure of our Government without recourse to the people themselves as provided in their own Constitution. This country belongs to the people, and it doesn't belong to any Administration.

Next, I suggest that they read their Oath of Office to support the Constitution of the United States. And I ask them to remember that they took that oath with their hands on the Holy Bible, thereby calling upon God Almighty Himself to witness their solemn promise. It is bad enough to disappoint us.

WASHINGTON OR MOSCOW

Sixth: I suggest that from this moment they resolve to make the Constitution the Civil Bible of the United States, and pay it the same civil respect and reverence that they would religiously pay the Holy Scripture, and I ask them to read from the Holy Scripture the Parable of the Prodigal Son and to follow his example.

Stop! Stop wasting your substance in a foreign land, and come back to your Father's house.

Now, in conclusion let me give this solemn warning. There can be only one Capitol, Washington or Moscow!

There can be only one atmosphere of government, the clear, pure, fresh air of free America, or the foul breath of Communistic Russia.

There can be only one flag, the Stars and Stripes, or the Red Flag of the Godless Union of the Soviet.

There can be only one National Anthem. The Star Spangled Banner or the Internationale.

There can be only one victor. If the Constitution wins, we win. But if the Constitution—stop. Stop there. The Constitution can't lose! The fact is, it has already won, but the news has not reached certain ears.

129

SOCIALIST NORMAN THOMAS CLAIMS GREAT VICTORIES FOR SOCIALISM UNDER BOTH DEMOCRATS AND REPUBLICANS

Norman Thomas was the Socialist candidate for President in 1928 and for every single election during the next twenty years. However, he never received more than 190,000 votes because he ran on the Socialist ticket and Americans have always despised socialism whenever it was labeled as such. Unfortunately, however, they had never been educated to recognize socialist principles if they bore no label. This made it possible for the last several administrations to restructure the country on socialist lines without the American people realizing it.

By 1953 Norman Thomas was jubilant. He wrote a pamphlet called, *Democratic Socialism* in which he stated that:

". . . here in America more measures once praised or denounced as socialist have been adopted than once I should have thought possible short of a socialist victory at the polls."

Under President Eisenhower, Norman Thomas still found reasons to be jubilant. In the *Congressional Record* for April 17, 1958 (p. A-3080) Norman Thomas is quoted as saying:

"The United States is making greater strides toward Socialism under Eisenhower than even under Roosevelt, particularly in the fields of Federal spending and welfare legislation."

By 1962 Norman Thomas summed up the whole situation as follows:

"The difference between Democrats and Republicans is: Democrats have accepted some ideas of Socialism cheerfully, while Republicans have accepted them reluctantly." (*Cleveland Plain Dealer,* October 19, 1962)

But whether the various administrations in Washington have been pushing Socialism "cheerfully" or "reluctantly," the facts clearly support the contention of Dr. Quigley in *Tragedy And Hope,* that the people of the United States are being rapidly collectivized, their Constitution emasculated, and the groundwork laid to transform the United States into the major industrial power base for a global society of totalitarian socialism.

INDEX

ACHESON, DEAN
  Member of CFR, 54
  UN delegate, 54
  White Paper on China, 54
  Withdraws defense of China, 77
  Leads to Korean War, 77
  Subversion in State Dept., 80
  Challenged by McCarthy, 83
  Bilderberg Conf., 110
  Picture, 81
ADLAI E. STEVENSON INSTITUTE
    OF INTERNATIONAL AFFAIRS
  Million dollar Ford Grant, 66
ALDRICH, ABBY
  Marries a Rockefeller, 17
ALDRICH, SENATOR NELSON
  Daughter marries Rockefeller, 17
  Morgan associate, 17
ALL SOUL'S COLLEGE
  Round Table at Oxford, 37
ALLY BETRAYED
  Book by David Martin, 74
  Betrayal of Yugo., 74
AMARASIA MAGAZINE
  Published by IPR, 46
  Offices raided by FBI, 46
  1,800 secret doc. found, 46
AMERICAN ASSEMBLY
  Interlocked with CFR, 54
  Financed by Wall Street, 54
AMERICAN ASSOCIATION OF UN
  Interlocked with CFR, 54
  Wall Street financed, 54
AMERICAN COMMUNICATIONS ASSN.
  Communist-directed union, 79
AMERICAN FRIENDS SERVICE COMMITTEE
  For recognition of Red China, 63
  Ford Foundation grant, 63
AMERICAN TELEPHONE AND TELEGRAPH
  Morgan controlled
AMERICANS FOR DEMOCRATIC ACTION
  Role in U.S. Government, 3
  Interlocked with CFR, 54
  Financed by Wall Street, 54
AMERICA'S RETREAT FROM VICTORY
  Book by Jos. McCarthy, 87
  On Gen. George C. Marshall, 87
ANDREW A. PIATT
  Treasury Department, 17
ANTI-COMMUNISM
  Ford Foundation opposes, 63
  Hollywood rally, 92
  Reaction, 93-95
  Supression of, 95-97
ANTI-DEFAMATION LEAGUE (ADL)
  Opposes conservatives, 8
ARMOUR, J. OGDEN
  Rockefeller agent, 19
ASCHBERG, OLAF
  Swedish banker, 41
  Financed Russian Revolution, 41
ASSOCIATION OF HELPERS
  Part of Secret Society, 30
ASTOR FAMILY
  Owner of London *Times,* 32
  Part of Secret Society, 32
  Finances Secret Society, 33
AUSTRALIA
  Secret Society in, 37
AYDELOTTE, FRANK
  Secret Society in U.S., 33

BAILEY, SIR ABE
  Finances Secret Society, 30-33
BAKER, BOBBY SCANDAL
  Press avoided, 102
  Not tied in to LBJ, 102
BAKER, GEORGE F.
  N. Y. financier, 19
BALFOUR, LORD ARTHUR
  In Secret Society, 30
BALL, GEORGE
  Nixon advisor, 55
  Member CFR, 55
  Bilderberg, 109
BANK OF ENGLAND
  Private organization, 12
  Influence in Britain, 13
BANKERS TRUST COMPANY
  Morgan firm, 23
BARING BANKING FAMILY
  Wealthy dynasty, 7
  In Bank of England, 13
BARING, (LORD CROMER)
  Gov. Bank of England, 14
BARUCH, BERNARD
  With Pres. Eisenhower, 19
  Backs Wilson, 19
  Picture, 19
BEAM, JACOB
  Nixon ambassador to USSR, 55
  Member CFR, 55
BEER, GEORGE LOUIS
  Secret Society in U.S., 33
  On American Round Table, 34
BEIT, ALFRED
  Finances Secret Society, 30
BEIT BANKING FAMILY
  In Secret Society, 33
BENDING OF THE TWIG
  Book by A. G. Rudd, 71
  Socialism in schools, 71
BENSON, DR. GEORGE S.
  Anti-Communist, 92
BERG, FRITZ
  Chairman, Fed. German Ind., 110
  Bilderberger, 110
BERNHARD, PRINCE
  Chairman, Bilderberger Group, 108-109
  Picture, 109
BILDERBERG CONFERENCES
  Interlocked with CFR, 54
  Background, 108-109
  Those who attend, 109-111
  Prince Bernhard, Chairman, 108
  Secret meeting, 108
BIRCHENOUGH, SIR HENRY
  Disciple of Ruskin, 29
  Member Secret Society, 30
BIRGI, M. MURI
  Turkish minister, 110
  Bilderberger, 110
BIRMINGHAM, STEPHEN
  Quoted, 16
BLACK REVOLUTION
  Financed by Ford Foundation, 65-66
BOWMAN, ISAIAH
  Officer of CFR, 34
BOZELL, L. BRENT
  Book on McCarthy, 87
BRAIN WASHING IN THE HIGH SCHOOLS
  Book by E. Merril Root, 71

131

INDEX

BRETT, REGINALD BALIOL (LORD ESHER)
Disciple of Ruskin, 29
Leader in Secret Society, 30
BROWDER, EARL
Sec. of Communist Party, 63
Employed by Fund for Rep., 62-63
BROWN BROTHERS BANKING FAMILY
Power in U.S., 16
BROWNELL, HERBERT JR.
Concerning H. D. White, 2
BUCHANAN, SIR GEORGE
Finances Soviet Revolution, 40
BUCKLEY, WILLIAM F.
Book on McCarthy, 87
BUNDY, McGEORGE
Graduate of Yale, 64
Employed by CFR, 64
Harvard dean at 34, 64
Advisor to JFK, 64
Advisor to LBJ, 64
Backs Reds in Dominican Republic, 64
Removal from government, 65
Pres. Ford Foundation, 65
Finances revolutionists, 65-66
Left-wing organization 66-67
Bilderberger, 109
Picture, 65
BUNKER, ELLSWORTH
Nixon ambassador to Saigon, 55
Member CFR, 55
BURNS, ARTHUR
Member of CFR, 55
Chairman Fed. Reserve, 55
Nixon Administration, 55
BUSINESS ADVISORY COUNCIL
Interlocked with CFR, 54
Financed by Wall St., 54
BURCH, DEAN
Quoted on Goldwater, 101-102
BURNS, WALTER
With J. P. Morgan, 9
BUTLER, NICHOLAS MURRAY
Pres. of Columbia, 36
Appointed through Morgan, 36, 69
Spokesman for Morgan, 70
IBM appointed successor, 70
CANADA
Org. of Secret Society in, 31
CANHAM, ERWIN D.
Secret Society, U.S., 33
Christian Science Monitor, 33
CARNEGIE ENDOWMENT FOR INT'L PEACE
Hiss connections with, 41
Promotes a war, 61
Sponsors Int'l Relations Clubs, 61
Finances Bilderbergers, 109
CARNEGIE FOUNDATION
Finances IPR, 44
Socialist Charter for Ed., 60
CENTER FOR THE STUDY OF
DEMOCRATIC INSTITUTIONS
Branch of Fund for Rep., 63
Financed by Ford Foundation, 63
Under Robert M. Hutchins, 63
CHAMBERLAIN, JOSEPH P.
Gov. of Bd. of IPR, 45
Columbia U., 45
CHAMBERS, WHITAKER
Admitted Communist, 41
Linked to Hiss, 58

CHAMBERS, WHITAKER, Cont.
FDR would not believe, 76
Senior editor of *Time*, 76
Author of *Witness*, 77
CHASE-MANHATTAN BANK
World banking power, 16
Finances IPR, 44
"CHATHAM HOUSE"
Secret Society hqts., 34
Near home of Astors, 34
"Chatham Group," 34
CHAING KAI SHEK
State Dept. Threat, 74
All Aid withdrawn, 74
CHINA
Role of IPR in fall, 44
Nixon adm. softening on, 56
Recognition of Red China, 63
Threat to Chiang, 74
U.S. withdraws aid, 74
Red Chinese in Korean War, 77
CHINA LOBBY (NATIONALIST CHINA)
Charges U.S. subversion, 47
Quigley admits charges, 47
CHISHOLM, DR. BROCK
World Mental Health, 116
CHRISTIAN SCIENCE MONITOR
Erwin D. Canham, 33
Articles by Lord Lothian, 37
Article on CFR, 51
CHRISTIANSON, HANKON
Danish business exec., 110
Bilderberger, 110
CHRISTMAS
Elimination from schools, 72
CHURCHES
Morgan influence over, 36
"CIRCLE OF INITIATES"
Part of Secret Society, 30
CLARK, KENNETH
Quoted 26-27
CLEVELAND, HARLAN
U.S. Ambassador to NATO, 55
Member CFR, 55
Nixon administration, 55
"CLIVEDEN SET"
Astor family home, 32
Meeting of Secret Society, 32
COLEGROVE, PROF. KENNETH
Attacks White Paper on China, 76
COLLECTIVISM ON THE CAMPUS
Book by E. Merril Root, 71
COLUMBIA UNIVERSITY
Influence of Morgan, 36
Morgan elects presidents, 36
Nicholas Murray Butler, 36, 69
IPR influence in, 45
Owen Lattimore from, 45
Jos. P. Chamberlain from, 45
Philip C. Jessup from, 45
Eisenhower as president, 69
Employment of M. Kridl, 70
Teachers College, 70
COMMIN, PIERRE
Sec. French Socialists, 110
Bilderberger, 110
COMMITTEE FOR ECONOMIC DEVELOP-
MENT
Interlock with CFR, 54
Financed by Wall Street, 54

132

136

INDEX

138

INDEX

MC ADOO, WILLIAM
  Sec. of Treasury, 21
  Wilson's son-in-law, 21
  Suspects Wall Street, 21
MC CARRAN COMMITTEE
  Hearings on fall of China, 44
  Blames IPR, 44
MC CARTHY AND HIS ENEMIES
  Book by Buckley and Bozell, 87
MC CARTHY
  Book by Roy Cohn, 82
  Background on McCarthy Hearings, 82
  Picture, 83
MC CARTHY, JOSEPH
  Background, 81-82
  Graduated from H. S., age 20, 81
  Degree in law Marquette U., 81
  Circuit judge, 82
  Enlisted in Marines, 82
  Military missions, 82
  Defeated Sen. Lafollette, 82
  Launches attack on subversives in U.S.
  State Department, 83
  Tydings Committee, 83
  Becomes Chairman of Senate Investiga-
  ting Committee, 84
  Results of 169 hearings, 84
  Clash with Gen. Zwicker, 85-86
  Charges against McCarthy, 87-89
  All dropped but two, 88
  Censure of McCarthy, 89
  Tragedy of "McCarthyism," 89
  Dr. Quigley on McCarthy, 89-91
  Picture, 83
MC CLOY, JOHN J.
  Morgan law firm, 37
  Head of Chase-Manhattan Bank, 54
  Member of CFR
  Delegate to UN conference, 54
  Bilderberger, 110
MC CRACKEN, DR. PAUL
  Nixon economics advisor, 55
  Member CFR, 55
MC DONALD, DAVID J.
  Pres. of United Steel Workers, 110
  Bilderberger, 110
MC KENNA, REGINALD
  Chancellor of Exchequer, 13
MC KISSICK, FLOYD
  Assoc. of Stokely Carmichael, 66
  Officer of CORE, 66
  Receives Ford grant, 66
NAKED COMMUNIST, THE
  Book by W. C. Skousen, 92
  Reaches best seller list, 92
NATIONAL CITIZENS LEAGUE
  Front to sell Fed. Reserve, 20
NATIONAL CITY BANK
  Financed CFR, 44
NATIONAL COMMITTEE ON U.S. CHINA
RELATIONS
  Given Ford Grant, 66
NATIONAL COUNCIL OF AMERICAN-
SOVIET FRIENDSHIP
  Corliss Lamont, chairman, 43
NATIONAL COUNCIL OF CHURCHES
  Strong Left-wing bias, 8
NATIONAL EDUCATION ASSOCIATION
  Not for traditional Am. Ed., 60

NATIONAL EDUCATION TEL. AND
RADIO CENTER (N.E.T.)
  6 million Ford grant, 67
NATIONAL PLANNING ASSOCIATION
  Interlocked with CFR, 54
  Financed by Secret Society, 54
NATIONAL STUDENT ASSOCIATION
  Ford grant, 66
NATIONAL URBAN LEAGUE
  Stops sup. of non-violence, 66
  Campaigns for Black Power, 66
  2 million Ford grant, 66
NEGRO
  Socialist study of, 60
"NETWORK" OF LONDON-NEW YORK
POWER
  See "Establishment of Global Power"
NEW MASSES
  Communist publication, 43
  F. V. Field on board, 43
NEW REPUBLIC MAGAZINE
  Founded by Willard Straight, 35
  Financed by Payne Whitney, 35
  Aimed at Left-wing, 35
  Walter Lippmann, editor, 35
"NEW RICH"
  Opposes "old rich," 106
  Goldwater campaign, 106-107
  Described as "ignorant," 106
NEW YORK TIMES
  Voice of Secret Society, 37
  Left-wing book reviews, 48
  Power behind it, 49
NEW YORK HERALD TRIBUNE
  Owned by J. H. Whitney, 35
  Morgan influence in, 37
  Voice of Establishment, 37
  Left-wing book reviews, 48
NEWSPAPERS OF ESTABLISHMENT
  New York Times, 37
  New York Herald Tribune, 37
  Christian Science Monitor, 37
  Washington Post, 37
  Boston *Evening Transcript,* 37
NEW ZEALAND
  Secret Society in, 33
NITZE, PAUL
  Sec. of Navy, 109
  Bilderberger, 109
  Would not expose secrets, 109
NIXON, RICHARD
  CFR domination of adm., 54-56
  CFR members on staff, 54-55
  Softening on China, 56
  Direct liaison with CFR, 55
  Picture, 56
NORMAN, MONTAGUE
  Bank of England, 23
  Friend of Ben. Strong, 23
OBSCENITY
  Judicial decisions on, 114
OFFICE OF ECONOMIC OPPORTUNITY
(OEO)
  Unionizing welfare clients, 66
OPPENHEIMER, J. ROBERT
  At Princeton Institute, 37
  Defended by Fund for Rep., 63
OSWALD, LEE HARVEY
  Member of Castro front, 98-99
  Assassinates Pres. Kennedy, 98

139

INDEX

140

INDEX

143